AM I ALLOWED TO CRY?

This book belongs to
Peter's Place.

Peter's Place
A Center for Grieving Children and Families

- distributed by -
Rainbow Connection
477 Hannah Branch Road
Burnsville, NC 28714
Phone: 704/675-5909

HUMAN HORIZONS SERIES

AM I ALLOWED TO CRY?

A Study of Bereavement amongst People who have Learning Difficulties

Maureen Oswin

A CONDOR BOOK
SOUVENIR PRESS (E&A) LTD

First published 1991 by Souvenir Press (Educational & Academic) Ltd,
43 Great Russell Street, London WC1B 3PA
and simultaneously in Canada

ISBN 0 285 65095 5 hardback
ISBN 0 285 65096 3 paperback

Phototypeset by Intype, London
Printed in Great Britain by
WBC Print and Binders Ltd
Bridgend, Glamorgan

AUTHOR'S NOTE

When the work for this book was begun, the term 'people with mental handicaps' was in use. In the late 1980s, however, that term was discontinued as being derogatory and labelling, and the phrase 'people with learning difficulties' was substituted. In parts of this book the earlier expression of 'mental handicap' is sometimes used. The author wishes to apologise if this give offence to anyone; the use is not meant to be demeaning but is used in an historical context only.

The United Kingdom is now a multi-racial society and the great religions of Islam, Hinduism, Judaism, and Buddhism are a part of British life. The author wishes to apologise for the discussions in this book being based only on Christian traditions of mourning.

The names used in this study are fictitious in order to protect the privacy of the people met, except for pages 137–40 where the story of Rodney Weeks occurs, which is printed by kind permission of Morag Lyddon.

ACKNOWLEDGEMENTS

The Joseph Rowntree Memorial Trust generously funded this research, and gave wonderfully kind support during the long process of completing it. I would like to thank the Trust for their generosity and patience; special thanks are also owed to Linda Ward, of the Joseph Rowntree Memorial Trust, for her very kind support and advice.

I also have to acknowledge with gratitude the immense help given by families, and the staff and residents of hospitals and hostels, and social workers and therapy staff in local health services and local social services departments; this book could not have been written without their willingness to give me their time. Special thanks are owed to Mr Rodney Weeks and Mrs Morag Lyddon for permission to quote the story on pages 137–40.

I would also like to thank Joan Rush of King's Fund Centre, and Joyce Knowles, the former principal of Castle Priory College, Wallingford, for their earlier support of this work through discussion and meetings from 1979 to 1983.

Finally I have to thank Sandra Stone of the Thomas Coram Research Unit, who gave invaluable secretarial help during the initial stages of organising the research in 1982, and Olwen Davies, also of Thomas

Coram Research Unit, who worked closely with me on
the manuscript and patiently took it through many
drafts and advised me on its format and contents.

I am grateful to the following for permission to quote
from copyright material: The Macmillan Press Ltd and
S. Lieberman for 'Living with Loss', published in *Post-
graduate Medical Journal*, October 1982; The Estate
of C. P. Cavafy and The Hogarth Press for 'Lovely
White Flowers' from *Collected Poems of C. P. Cavafy*,
translated by Edmund Keeley and Philip Sherrard;
Routledge for *Loss and Change* by Peter Marris; *The
British Journal of Psychiatry* and Colin Murray-
Parkes for 'Bereavement'; Curtis Brown on behalf of
The Estate of Mary Renault for *The Charioteer* Copy-
right Mary Renault 1953; *Mental Retardation* and
Lotte E. Moise for 'In sickness and in death'. The
extract from 'Niobe' by Aeschylus, translated by
C. M. Bowra, from the *Oxford Book of Greek Verse in
translation* edited by T. F. Higham and C. M. Bowra, is
reproduced by permission of Oxford University Press.
Quotations from *Kathleen* by E. M. Blaiklock and
*Letter to My Husband: Notes about Mourning and
Recovery* by Jill Truman are reproduced by permission
of Hodder & Stoughton Ltd/New English Library Ltd.

CONTENTS

INTRODUCTION

This book is about grief and the sort of things that can happen to bereaved people if they have a learning difficulty; it looks at how their adjustment to loss is helped or hindered by the people who come into contact with them and the services which they are offered, and by general attitudes towards disability or learning difficulties.

My awareness of the problems of bereaved mentally handicapped people began in the early 1970s when I was visiting long-stay hospitals where people with multiple disabilities were living permanently. In my book *Holes in the Welfare Net** I referred to bereavement as follows:

> In the garden of a large mental handicap hospital, a thin, tall, middle-aged woman stood apart from the other women; she was holding a large, brown knitted doll, and looked full of despair. The long legs of the doll were held over the woman's hips, her hands were clasped behind its back; she looked down onto its soft shapeless face and moved her lips, then lifted it and kissed it.
>
> The staff explained that this woman had only been living in the hospital for six months. She had come

* Published by Bedford Square Press (1978), London.

when both her elderly parents had died within a few months of each other and there was nobody else to look after her. 'It's about time she got over it,' a member of the staff said. 'She won't do anything and she won't be separated from that old doll. She brought that from home. We don't mind her having it, of course, but it reminds her of home too much. She should be over all that by now, as she's got quite a lot of sense.' (page 102).

In the summaries and suggestions at the end of that book I wrote:

Helping bereaved mentally handicapped people. This is a sadly neglected area of need, requiring careful research into what is now happening to these people, and an exploration of ways in which they may be helped.

(Ibid, page 156).

Soon after the publication of that book I had a phone call from Joyce Knowles, then the principal of Castle Priory College, Wallingford (a college run by the Spastics Society and at that time having a special interest in courses for staff working in long-stay institutions). Joyce had read my description of the grieving woman and she said that she would like to organise a course at Castle Priory to help staff to understand more about bereavement. But as we talked we both agreed that we ourselves needed to learn more about the problems before we organised a course.

So we gathered a group of interested people and over the next two years we met regularly at the King's Fund Centre under the auspices of Mrs Joan Rush, to talk about how people with learning difficulties could get more understanding and appropriate help when they were bereaved. In 1980 the King's Fund group produced a small leaflet called *The Right to Grieve*, and in December 1981 the Fund published my booklet called *Bereavement and Mentally Handicapped People*.

In 1982 I began this research study, which was kindly funded by the Joseph Rowntree Memorial Trust. The aim was to look in more detail at some of the aspects of bereavement brought to the fore by the work of the King's Fund group. However, ironically, the research was dogged from the start by my own personal bereavements. A few weeks after I began the work in 1982 my mother died. This was a great blow to me and I felt very upset when interviewing some of the bereaved families whom I had arranged to visit.

Then, in 1983, my widowed sister was diagnosed as having brain cancer. Her prognosis was very poor and I gave up the work in order to care for her. She lived until 1988 but needed a great deal of care; with the help of district nurses and other community services I managed to nurse her myself and she died at home with me. The Joseph Rowntree Memorial Trust were wonderfully supportive through the years that I was nursing my sister, and they agreed that the research should be suspended until I could take up the work again.

In my sad years of 1982–1988, following the death of my mother and then nursing my sister through her long dying, as I felt my own grief and saw all the grieving people in the cancer hospital which my sister attended for her treatment, I thought that it sometimes seems as if all our lives we are trying to cope with loss – either the fear of it, or the memory of it, or its raw immediate presence.

In grief we veer from coping to not coping, from vivid clear memories to surprise at forgetting. One of the mothers I met when I was writing this book described her son as 'watching the door for his father for months after he died'. We do 'watch the door' for a long time when we are bereaved, as we gradually learn to know that the dead person will never again come back to us. And after a while, as we gradually put aside our grief, we have times when we almost want to hold on to it and cherish it, for it seems to be the last thing belonging to the person we miss, and in putting our grief away we feel that we are finally placing the dead person firmly in the past.

This book offers no solution to grief, for there is none. W. B. Yeats wrote:

> Man is in love
> And loves what vanishes;
> What more is there to say?

However, knowing that we cannot solve grief, nor prevent it, knowing that it is the price we pay for our attachment to others, we can still hope not to make it worse; especially not worse for people who are already vulnerable because they are lonely, or very young or very old, or sick, or handicapped in some way. With this aim I have written this book, and it asks two questions: how can we make sure that the tender feelings of people with learning difficulties, and their families, and their staff, are treated with sensitivity? And how can we plan services so that they do not make sad people sadder?

1 HOW IS IT TO GRIEVE?

> The death of a loved one is one of the most stress-
> ful events of our lives. During our subsequent
> reactions we can experience sensations, dream
> dreams, feel emotions and believe in ways which
> may lead us to question our morals, faith and
> sanity.
>
> Stuart Lieberman (1982)[1]

A loss through death provokes the three most pitiful
of human emotions: grief, mourning and pining.
Poetry and literature over the centuries have
attempted to explain the mystery of death and to
describe the feelings of mourning people: Aeschylus
(525–456 BC) writes chillingly of man's helplessness
against the power of death:

> Alone of gods Death has no love for gifts,
> Libation helps you not, nor sacrifice.
> He has no altar, and he hears no hymns;
> From him alone Persuasion stands apart.
> (from 'Niobe')[2]

St Augustine (AD 354–430) writing on the loss of a
friend, expresses the wretchedness of his bereavement:

> At this grief my heart was utterly darkened; and what-
> ever I beheld was death ... Mine eyes sought him

everywhere, but he was not granted them; and I hated
all places, for they had not him . . . [3]

It is not unusual to feel that life is no longer worth
living, that memory itself is too hard to bear and that
all the familiar places enjoyed with the dead person
have become saddened and dead places, and even hate-
ful to visit. The Greek poet C. P. Cavafy (1863–1933)
wrote:

> He laid flowers on his cheap coffin
> lovely white flowers, very much in keeping
> with his beauty, his twenty-two years.
>
> When he went to the café that evening –
> he happened to have some vital business there –
> to that same café where they used to go together,
> it was a knife in his heart,
> that dead café where they used to go together.
>
> (from 'Lovely White Flowers').[4]

Dora Carrington (1893–1932) grieved beyond all bal-
ance by the death of Lytton Strachey, wrote of how
life had lost all purpose for her:

> . . . they say one must keep your standards and your
> values of life alive. But how can I, when I only kept
> them for you? . . . I dreamt of you again last night.
> And when I woke up it was as if you had died afresh.
> Every day I find it *harder* to bear. For what point is
> there in life now? . . . It is impossible to think that I
> shall never sit with you again and hear you laugh.
> *That every day for the rest of my life you will be away.*
>
> (February 1932, entry in diary).[5]

She wrote thus, in utter despair a few weeks after
Lytton Strachey had died in January 1932, and,

unable to bear her life without him, suffering inconsolable grief, she killed herself in March 1932.

Caitlin Thomas, the widow of the poet Dylan Thomas, wrote a book after his death. Its terse title, *Leftover Life to Kill*,[6] expresses the grief of widowhood.

In the pain of grieving for the recently dead, bereaved people do often feel that life has nothing more to offer them; as, tragically, the brilliant and sensitive Dora Carrington felt. They cannot believe that 'time will heal'. That hackneyed phrase is horrible to them, a betrayal of the dead person whom they loved so much. E. M. Blaiklock, in his gentle book *Kathleen*, wrote of how the grief caused by his widowhood could assail him afresh more than a year after his wife died:

> It was when I entered the empty house in the early afternoon that the desolation of life without her enveloped me like a shroud. If anyone ever reads this it will be perhaps to despise my frailty, rather than to understand how, after fifty-eight weeks, I can still sob and call to her. The grief will not abate, nor transform itself, though in truth I have offered it to God for such an alchemy.[7]

Grief can make a person feel frightened, weak, angry, physically sick, exhausted, and very vulnerable. C. S. Lewis wrote, 'No one ever told me that grief is so like fear, the same fluttering in the stomach, the same restlessness . . .'[8]

We express grief in a variety of ways, some of which are easily recognisable as mourning: we cry, look dejected, seem to age suddenly, get depressed, are unable to summon the energy to do even simple tasks, we cannot sleep. Other ways of grieving may not be so easily recognised, such as getting quickly angry, being excited or irritable, or oddly controlled and seeming to have no feelings at all; strangely, too, we may even laugh excessively and suddenly think an ordinary or even sombre scene is very comical.

In our grief we may also lose some of our abilities, so that simple tasks such as writing a shopping list, putting out a note for the milkman, signing a cheque, using the phone, making a cup of tea, may seem difficult. We may say to friends, 'You do it please, I'm knocked sideways,' or, 'I cannot think straight.' It seems as if the enormity of our loss, the immense strange experience of death, fills all our conscious thought and action, and leaves no room for anything else.

Grief can disturb our sense of time; we are loath to sunder immediately our relationship with the person who has died, our joint habits, and their part in our identity, so we may search for them as we take time emotionally and physically to accept our separation from them. This does not mean that we actually look upstairs and expect to find them, but we have a tenuous wish to resurrect the identity we had when that person was alive and which their death has diminished. For when anybody dies we also die a little or change a little, and it takes time to be that diminished or new person. So, on our own, quietly at home, we may get comfort from pretending that they will be found again in the familiar places; we may softly call their names or say 'goodnight' to them, we may look out of the window and imagine them coming along the road, open the wardrobe to see if their clothes are there, look at the bed to imagine them there again, expect their knock on the door and their footsteps on the stairs. This is normal behaviour, for in the early days of somebody having died we know that it has happened but we want to disbelieve the finality of death. It is as if we *need* to enact their existence, and need to search for them, in order to help ourselves slowly to realise their death and gradually let go and accept their irrevocable absence and our own changed identity.

Some bereaved writers have gained comfort themselves, and given support to others, by writing a 'letter' to the dead person. Jill Truman in her book *Letter to My Husband* writes:

> My dear love, tomorrow it will be exactly four months since you died. It seems like forty years since I have been battling on alone, and yet your presence is so vivid that I expect at any moment to hear your key turn in the lock and your loud familiar voice calling 'hello' as you stride along the hallway. With what joy we would all rush to greet you, because no man was ever more loved than you, you old bastard.[9]

and:

> What does it mean to be dead? I cannot accept that you are totally annihilated. All that passion, all that restless striving and enthusiasm – gone. (*ibid*)

And later:

> And what do I say to our little Rebecca when she weeps and weeps and says 'I want my daddy'? I want her daddy, too. You don't stop loving and wanting someone just because they are dead. You can't be dead. There's been some terrible mistake. Tomorrow you will come back and we'll all laugh about it. (*ibid*)

and:

> There are some nights when I can't write. Nothing is possible but grief. (*ibid*)

Thus Jill Truman writes a long and moving letter to

her dead husband, eloquently and with great sensitivity capturing the awful mixture of emotions one feels after somebody dies: the disbelief, the instability, the veering between anger, weakness, panic, exhaustion, courage and sheer misery.

The normality of grief

All the reactions mentioned above (for instance, tears, laughter, loss of abilities, dejection) are very common after losing somebody through death. We may feel them all in the space of a day, and to other people we may seem quite difficult and even rather unstable. But our feelings and behaviour are normal emotional reactions to loss.

In the last thirty years there has been considerable documentation of research into grief in western society. Research findings, describing emotions which parallel those found also in the early poetry and literature of death, suggest that there are recognisable *normal patterns and stages in grieving*.

Peter Marris writes of typical signs of grief:

> The typical signs of grief can be summarised, then, as physical distress and worse health; an inability to surrender the past – expressed, for instance, by brooding over memories, sensing the presence of the dead, clinging to possessions, being unable to comprehend the loss, feelings of unreality; withdrawal into apathy; and hostility against others, against fate, or turned in upon oneself.[10]

And describes the behaviour of bereaved people:

> The behaviour of the bereaved is characteristically ambivalent; they may be desperately lonely, yet shun company; they may try to escape reminders of their loss, yet cultivate memories of the dead; they complain

if people avoid them, embarrassed how to express their sympathy, yet rebuff that sympathy irritably when it is offered. (*ibid*)

Colin Murray-Parkes refers to 'pangs of grief':

> There are episodes of restlessness, angry pining, and anxiety, brought on by any reminders of the loss, and including the automatic accompaniments of anxiety and fear . . . the fact that the intelligent human adult knows very well that it is useless to cry aloud and to search for the dead person does not remove the impulse to do just that.[11]

And concerning 'recovery':

> Because each relationship is different, each grief is different, and it is not possible to adopt a rigid time frame for bereavement. Also, there is no clear end to grief. The bereaved do not forget the past: rather, they gradually discover which assumptions continue to be relevant and enriching in their new life situation and which have to be abandoned. However, the old assumptive world remains in the mind – a network of associations into which the bereaved can again be switched by anything which brings the dead person to mind. (*ibid*)

Stuart Lieberman refers to the inevitability of the pain of bereavement:

> Explanation of the feelings which we suffer when separation and loss occur begins with a central truth. Our feelings after a loss are the price we pay for our attachment to other people.[1]

Since the 1950s there has been a growth in bereavement counselling services through local hospitals and local authority social service departments, hospices and community hospice teams. Foremost amongst the voluntary associations which are concerned with understanding and helping people who are bereaved are CRUSE (founded 1959) and the Compassionate Friends (founded 1969). The former was set up initially to help widows, but now helps all groups of bereaved people; the latter organisation gives support specifically to people who have suffered the death of a child. Both organisations offer befriending on a one-to-one basis or through group meetings. They also issue newsletters and have a range of advisory literature. CRUSE provides training courses for those who work professionally or in a lay capacity with bereaved people.

It would seem that there have been considerable developments in the understanding of grief, and that the majority of professionals and voluntary groups try to make wise use of documented research when organising support for bereaved people. Ultimately, however, one's recovery from loss is a lonely personal struggle, for each person's grief is individual, unique, strange and frightening. In addition, our grief and the manner and extent to which we mourn are not entirely encapsulated in the death which has been recently experienced; our personal identity is also involved. Our past, our need for security, our previous experiences of loss and our recognition of our own mortality, will all have a part in our mourning and our recovery.

Why should people with learning difficulties have special problems in bereavement?
Throughout the 1970s the development of services for people with learning difficulties was quite rightly influenced by the philosophy of 'normalisation', that is, the premise that people who have physical disabilities or learning difficulties, or who are disadvantaged

in any one way or in multiple ways, are, in spite of these difficulties, eligible for all the advantages or disadvantages of ordinary living facilities, in housing, health care, education, recreation, employment and retirement. This means that people with learning difficulties, who were in the 1970s generally described as 'mentally handicapped' (and before that often labelled as 'retarded', 'idiots', 'imbeciles', 'morons' or 'mongols') should have equal right to ordinary good housing instead of living in institutions, should have access to general hospital facilities, should have education in ordinary schools under local education authorities, should be able to make friends, have sexual relationships, marry if they wish, obtain employment, be able to enjoy a variety of recreational facilities, and have appropriate support when elderly.

In the last ten years, due to ceaseless campaigns by concerned individuals and organisations, some of these normal aims have been achieved, that is, many children with learning difficulties are receiving their education in ordinary local schools, some of the large old hospitals which once housed a thousand or more 'patients' have been shut, and many of their former residents are living in ordinary housing. The study of these achievements in ordinary living has been documented by the Long-term Team of the King's Fund Centre,[12] the staff of which have been actively involved in influencing policy changes.

Crucial to the campaigns for people with learning difficulties to have access to ordinary facilities has been the changing of attitudes in society. For example, some die-hard professionals (doctors, nurses, social workers) resisted the suggestion that their 'patients' could ever live outside a mental handicap hospital; some parents of people with learning difficulties feared the consequence of what they felt was going to be lack of supervision for their 'children' (many of whom were aged thirty or forty years old); some sections of the public, not having met any people with learning difficulties, were nervous about the closure of hospitals, imagining that people from hospitals would be difficult or even dangerous neighbours. But over the last decade much has been achieved in changing professional and parental and public attitudes, and it is now generally accepted that people with learning difficulties do have a right to be as independent as possible.

However, despite all the advances made in changing attitudes towards people with learning difficulties, it appears that in the area of loss and bereavement they are still not receiving enough consideration, nor the appropriate support that they require.

Basically, this shortfall is due to:

a) emphatically bad attitudes to people with learning difficulties, which has meant that their bereavement problems have been largely ignored, for example, 'they do not have the same feelings as the rest of us'.

and

b) death and grief creates fears and uncertainties for most people, and the combination of bereavement *and* people with learning difficulties, a double taboo, has usually been considered so fraught that the problems have been swept under the carpet.

Either way, it has meant that many people with learning difficulties are not always appropriately supported when they are bereaved, and they may even be given extra problems which are due not to their handicaps but to the way in which other people regard them and seek to manage their lives without always consulting them or even informing them about decisions. They are frequently at the receiving end of bad decisions made for them by people who do not know them, and they may have additional losses piled on top of the primary loss. For example, sometimes they are moved out of a family home immediately after a parent dies, so they also suffer the loss of home, possessions, local friends, pets, even their own clothes.

If they are living in a residential setting or attending a day centre where the staff do not understand the normality of instability caused by grief, any upset that they show may be seen only in terms of their 'mental handicap' and not be recognised as normal grief. However, there is no reason to assume that people who have learning difficulties will not have the same reactions to loss that more able people have. The difference for them is that their reactions are not always recognised as normal, partly because staff may be inexperienced in their knowledge of bereavement, or because their whole approach to the person with a learning difficulty concentrates on abnormality rather than normality.

Sometimes, bereaved people with learning difficulties are not only whisked off into a residential care placement which is not familiar to them, but they are not even told what has happened to their homes and their own personal belongings that they have left behind them and they may never return to their original home or neighbourhood. And if their grief reactions are not recognised by the staff in the residential care placement they will grieve alone and misunderstood, at the same time as having to make adjustments to a new environment and to living amongst strangers. It is a wonder that they survive at all. Indeed some do not survive, they never really recover their emotional strength and happiness, and never manage to cope with the massive changes and losses they have experienced; they potter along in the remaining years of their lives, quiet, pining, easily upset.

The aim of this book is to draw attention to the special problems of being bereaved when also having learning difficulties. These special problems may be related to having restricted language or a massive language disorder, so that they cannot talk about their grief; or may be related to having additional physical disabilities which makes them very dependent on other people for all their care. A person with severe multiple physical handicaps may be blind, speechless and paralysed and thus completely dependent on other people. Their bereavement will be a major physical shock as well as an emotional shock; after the death of a caring parent they may have to live in a completely new environment, surrounded by new and strange sounds, lights, smells and textures, being fed their food by strangers, being lifted by people whose voices and hands are unfamiliar. This may be very frightening to them.

Some people with learning difficulties may be given all sorts of peculiar ideas about what has happened, perhaps being told that the dead person has 'gone away', or 'gone to sleep'. Such explanations will be very frightening and terrible, especially if they have recently had an argument with the person who has died; they may think that the disappearance is connected with them having been 'difficult'. Inarticulate and verbally handicapped people are also unable to get comfort by receiving, reading and answering letters of sympathy, a task which often helps by re-affirming the loss and placing the dead person in a new perspective.

They may want to discuss what has happened and go over it again and again (a very normal reaction) but may find themselves instantly in a residential home or hospital where the staff cope with bereavement by trying to 'jolly' the person along. Flight into jollity is a common way of dealing with bereavement, and if the person with a learning difficulty cannot assert themselves, cannot assert their own grief and insist that they wish to mourn and have a right to be miserable, then they may well find themselves facing a barrage of jolly activities in the months immediately following their loss (see pages 99–100, Chapter 3).

Sometimes they are not told the truth about a death because it is thought that they will 'not understand' or 'will start fussing' or 'cause difficulties' for the other members of their family or other residents in the institution. Sometimes when they have to move out of the family home because of the death of a parent their *double loss of parent and home* will never be acknowledged as a major trauma.

People who are already living in hospitals are sometimes told 'you won't be visited any more' after a parent dies, and they may connect this with punishment or rejection. When the bereaved person also has a major physical disability and cannot speak they may *never* be told about the death; this may be because somebody in charge of their care makes a deliberate decision not to tell them 'in case it upsets them', but it may be because it never occurred to anyone to sit down beside them and explain that a parent or friend has died and hold them and comfort them as they need to be held and comforted.

Pressure is sometimes put on people with learning difficulties because the staff caring for them thought-

lessly link the death to some long-term problem that
the person has, for example:

'Your mum is dead; now you must be grown up and
not wet the bed any more';

or

'. . . now your mum's passed on you'll have to learn
to feed yourself';

or

'. . . you'll have to start dressing yourself on your
own now';

or

'now your father has passed away you must be
grown up and be the man of the house and help your
mother and stop behaving like a baby'.

These subtle condemnations and threats are unnecessary when a person is bereaved, and can only add to
their unhappiness and worries.

An inability to recognise the person's grief will
make them lonely at the very time that they need
other people and love and friendship. They not only
need their grief recognised, they also need permission
to grieve, especially if they live in a large institution
where so many of the activities that take place are a
sort of whipped-up happiness. It would seem that a
flight into jollity is often used as a means of stifling
grief by staff who do not know how to help bereaved
people (see above).

When people with learning difficulties are bereaved
they begin with so many disadvantages, due to their
position in society, to other people's low expectations
of them and the tendency to stereotype them and
regard them as 'objects of pity', or 'like children' and
needing protection from normality. A variety of people
may come into contact with them when they are newly
bereaved, who may have little or no sympathy for their

needs as a mourning person. For example, the family doctor and the district nurses and neighbours may know them, but not necessarily understand or respect that they are just as bereaved as the other members of the family.

Sometimes a death brings into the family home a number of people who are not known very well or not at all, but who are essential for the arrangements which have to be made after a death: for example, the undertaker, the family doctor, church minister, perhaps even the police if the death has been very sudden. What are their attitudes towards the person with a learning difficulty? Do they include them in the breaking of the news, do they show them the same respect as they show to other members of the family, do they even speak to them? The parents who shared in the research referred to some health and social service professionals ignoring the mentally handicapped member of the family when they visited the house at the time of the death, and even advising that they should be kept out of the way.

The majority of undertakers' staff are trained to offer respect and sympathy at the same time as conducting the necessary formalities of funerals, and therefore they will, hopefully, accord all members of the family an equal degree of compassion. But does the undertaker respect that the person with a learning difficulty also has a right to grieve? In organising the funeral, do they assume that they will not be attending it? Do they make it easy or hard for the family to include them in all the proceedings? Difficulties may arise if the person is very physically handicapped; how do undertakers cope with these problems? Do they include them in the cars for mourners, help them into the church and to the graveside or the crematorium?

Or do the difficulties seem so unsurmountable that the undertaker and the family mourners automatically exclude the person from the proceedings and thereby deny them the right to participate in the quiet display of mourning which is traditional in western society?

The family may be churchgoers, in which case the vicar or minister will hopefully know and respect the feelings of the family member who has a learning difficulty. But how does a minister or vicar behave when not knowing the person? Do they give advice that is appropriate to the needs of the grieving person who also has a learning difficulty? Do they encourage them to be included in the church service? Or do they suggest that they should be sent away on the day of the funeral?

Neighbours who have been close to a family for many years often provide the best source of help to the family in the days immediately following the bereavement. However, some neighbours take an unsympathetic, or even a punitive attitude towards the son or daughter who has a learning difficulty and have been known to make within their hearing such remarks as 'the death wouldn't have occurred if he/she had not had all that worry with that mentally handicapped person all these years', and similar.

Sometimes a very sentimental attitude is taken towards the person who has learning difficulties when they are bereaved. One woman, aged nearly thirty, was showered with presents for several months after her mother died. She received presents from all the staff at her day centre, the cleaners, office staff, other parents of handicapped people, the escort on the coach that took her each day to the day centre, and her neighbours. She was overwhelmed and excited by these gifts of sweets, clothes and flowers and money and eventually got confused about whether it was Christmas, her birthday or the death of her mother.

The two questions which should concern anyone connected with bereaved people with learning difficulties are: first, are their *normal grief reactions* being recognised as *normal?* Second, have the changes in their lives, which the bereavement has caused, been managed with wisdom, compassion and sensitivity?

There is very little literature on the special problems facing people who have learning difficulties when they are bereaved. In papers so far published there has been interesting discussion on the concepts of death about people with learning difficulties (E. Bihm and L. Eliot 1982[13]); on neurosis and stress, a major cause of their stress being the death of a parent (K. Day, 1985[14]); and several small but relevant and helpful studies of groups of people in institutions and day centres (J. Strachan, 1981;[15] K. Brelstaff, 1984[16]).

Literature suggests that there is a need for greater understanding and better organised services regarding the problem of bereaved people with learning difficulties (I. J. McLoughlin, 1986;[17] J. Bicknell, 1980;[18] M. Oswin, 1981,[19] 1982,[20] 1985[21] and 1988;[22] D. A. Kloeppel and S. Hollins[23]).

A selection of published case studies and personal accounts by professionals and relatives makes thoughtful and sometimes sad reading (J. Bradford, 1984;[24] B. McMasters, 1984;[25] R. Ray, M. Payne and M. Straker, 1978;[26] S. Jones, 1985[27]).

The following extract from a paper by a parent is a cogent argument for a more appropriate and sympathetic approach:

Barbara is twenty-three now. She has been living away from home for five years, and some of her friends have already lost their mothers or fathers. '. . . What is going to happen to me when you die?' she exploded like a bomb over her breakfast Cheerios on a recent weekend at home. 'And who's going to live in our house?' She had never said 'when' before — never apparently considered the issue of the house in which we have lived ever since she can remember. It seemed that she had suddenly taken a tremendous step towards acknowledging death as an inevitable part of the human condition.

We are immensely relieved, for my husband and I are trying to prepare and strengthen her for a future without us — not only in practical survival skills, but in essential emotional strengths.

It is rough going without them. Recently a lady in a group home for adults with mental retardation lost her elderly father. A new staff person asked the resident nurse for advice: 'How can I help Jane? She is all broken up with grief . . .' 'Oh, just give her a tranquilliser!' was the reply.

What a repressive, unfeeling way of coping with pain. What blatant denial of humanness to buffer that young woman's grief with a pill! What actions could we and should we take to prepare children and young people with mental retardation for the unavoidable dark side of our lives — sickness and inevitable death?

(Lotte E. Moise, 1978).[28]

It would seem that the literature to date on bereavement and people with learning difficulties falls into two schools of thought: first, that which seeks to define their developmental level and decide whether their concept of loss is child-like, whether they are less troubled by death because they lack understanding or more troubled because they are confused in their concepts; and second, that which points to the social and emotional needs of bereaved people with learning difficulties and considers their problems from a view of normal human grief reactions, and recommends that services should be appropriate and that staff should have opportunities to gain greater understanding of the problems via basic training and in-service training.

Both schools of thought have much to offer in improving the present situation for bereaved people who have learning difficulties and in answering the questions of how much is understood and recognised of their grief and, after recognition, what exactly is being done to support them through the difficult times.

The following chapters about families and institutional care suggest that all is not yet right regarding what is happening to people with learning difficulties when they are bereaved.

REFERENCES

1 LIEBERMAN, S., 'Living with loss', in *Postgraduate Medical Journal*, October 1982, **58**, 24–8.

2 AESCHYLUS, 'Niobe' from 'Inexorable Death', trans. C. M. Bowra, in *Oxford Book of Greek Verse in translation*, ed. T. F. Higham and C. M. Bowra (Oxford University Press, 1938).

3 AUGUSTINE, from *Confession* trans. E. B. Pusey (J. H. Parker, Oxford, 1838).

4 CAVAFY, C. P., 'Lovely White Flowers' from *Collected Poems of C. P. Cavafy*, trans. Edmund Keeley and Philip Sherrard (Hogarth Press, London, 1975).

5 *Carrington: Letters and extracts from her diaries*, ed. David Garnett (Jonathan Cape, London, 1970).

6   THOMAS, Caitlin, *Leftover Life to Kill* (Putnam, New York, 1957).

7   BLAIKLOCK, E. M., *Kathleen* (Hodder & Stoughton, London, 1980).

8   LEWIS, C. S., *A Grief Observed* (Faber & Faber, London, 1961).

9   TRUMAN, Jill, *Letter to my Husband: Notes about Mourning and Recovery* (Hodder & Stoughton, London, 1988).

10   MARRIS, Peter, *Loss and Change* (Institute of Community Studies, Routledge and Kegan Paul, London, 1974).

11   MURRAY-PARKES, C., 'Bereavement', in *British Journal of Psychiatry*, 1985, **146**, 11–17.

12   KING'S FUND CENTRE, An Ordinary Life Project Series (King's Fund, London):
People First (Linda Ward), Project Paper 37, November 1981.
An Ordinary Life, Project Paper 24, June 1982.
Planning for People (Linda Ward), Project Paper 47, April 1984.

13   BIHM, E., and ELIOT, L. 'Concept of death in mentally retarded persons', in *British Journal of Psychology*, 1982, III, 205–10.

14   DAY, K., 'Psychiatric disorder in middle-aged and the elderly mentally handicapped', in *British Journal of Psychiatry*, 1985, **147**, 665–8.

15   STRACHAN, J., 'Reactions to bereavement: a study of a group of adult mentally handicapped hospital residents', in *APEX*, Journal of the British Institute of Mental Handicap, 1981, **9**, 1, 20–1.

16   BRELSTAFF, K., 'Reactions to death: can the mentally handicapped grieve? Some experiences of those who did', in *Journal of National Association*

of *Teachers of Mentally Handicapped People*, May 1984, 10–17.

17 McLoughlin, I. J., 'Care of the dying: bereavement in the mentally handicapped', in *British Journal of Hospital Medicine*, October 1986, 256–60.

18 Bicknell, J., 'The Psychopathology of handicap', in *British Journal of Medical Psychology*, 1983, **56**, 167–78.

19 Oswin, M., *Bereavement and Mentally Handicapped People* (King's Fund, London (KFC 81/234), 1981).

20 Oswin, M., 'Nobody for me to look after', in *Parents' Voice*, March 1982, 10.

21 Oswin, M., 'Bereavement', Ch. 17 in *Mental Handicap: a multi-disciplinary approach*, ed. M. Craft, J. Bicknell and S. Hollins (Baillière Tindall, London, 1985).

22 Oswin, M., 'Bereavement and mentally handicapped people', Ch. 10 in *Last Things: Social Work with the Dying and Bereaved*, ed. T. Philpot (Community Care, Wallington, 1989).

23 Kloeppel, D. A., and Hollins, S., 'Double handicap: mental retardation and death in the family', in *Death Studies*, 1989, **13**, 31–8.

24 Bradford, J., 'Life after death', in *Parents' Voice*, May 1984, 6–7.

25 McMasters, B., 'It fell to me to break the news', in *Community Care*, April 1984, 25.

26 Ray, R., Payne, M., and Straker, M., 'They only live for today', in *Parents' Voice*, June 1978, 10–12.

27 Jones, S., 'George from Liverpool', in *Letters of l'Arche*, quarterly journal of the International

Federation of L'Arche, December 1985, 46 (Life Together), 7–9.

28   Moise, Lotte E., 'In sickness and in death', in *Mental Retardation*, December 1978, **16**, 6, 397–8.

2 FAMILIES

What I'd like to be sure of is that my son will
have a chance to make a close relationship with
somebody when I am no longer here, that is the
most important thing to me.

A parent

Bereavement makes many demands. Newly widowed
persons not only have their grief and intolerable missing of the dead person, but they also have to cope with
the difficult task of adapting to a solitary life, being
responsible for the household jobs and decision-taking
previously shared with their partner, and trying to
continue on their own the things which they once
enjoyed together. Some widows dread going out: 'it's
no pleasure on my own'; 'people are nice but I feel
different', they say. It is not only 'feeling different';
going out and being on one's own in company also
accentuates the loneliness, and this is renewed in
double measure when they return home afterwards to
the empty house. No wonder that it sometimes seems
better not to go out at all than to struggle and suffer
the lonely return. Adapting to their changed personal
circumstances requires immense effort and courage.
Nobody can disengage from a close relationship

quickly, the bereaved person needs time to recover and settle into a different life.

When there is a person in the family who has very severe learning difficulties, the new widow's adjustment to loss may be made more difficult because of practical problems related to their care, such as lifting them single-handed, or managing a heavy wheelchair up and down steps. However, widows frequently find that their sons or daughters with learning difficulties give them good support and that it is other people's prejudices about mental handicap which create the biggest problems. When Mrs Wilson was suddenly widowed she was worried about the best way to tell her son, and a social worker and a doctor told her not to tell him as 'it would be best if he doesn't know for the moment as you don't want any more problems on your plate.'

The professionals gave Mrs Wilson this insensitive advice because they underestimated her son's ability to feel the same emotions as other people and to support his mother during her grief. They assumed that as he had a learning difficulty he would not understand and would be difficult if he was told that his father had died. Her son was a gentle, sensible man aged twenty-four who had been devoted to his father, but for several weeks Mrs Wilson acted on the professionals' advice and let him think that his father was still in hospital. This secret, and the knowledge that she would eventually have to tell him, caused her immense strain during the early weeks of her bereavement and added considerably to her own loneliness and distress. The delay in telling her son also cut them off from each other when they most needed each other's loving help. She realised later on how unwise she had been not to tell her son the truth, but at the time she had been very vulnerable and felt that she should implicitly obey the professionals' advice.

Mrs Wilson's experience is not uncommon. The following quotations are taken from widows' letters. All the widows had sons or daughters with learning difficulties living at home, and their letters describe the struggles they had when they were first bereaved.

> My husband died 5 years ago just as we were getting ready to go out. I got in touch with social services to get my mentally handicapped daughter away for the funeral for two days. The following year a woman at my daughter's Day Centre died and the supervisor there asked if my daughter would like to go to the service. He was taking a lot of them so I agreed. When she came home that day I asked if she was all right and what did she think of the service, she was quite pleased she had gone. Then I thought if I'd known or realised I would have let her come to her father's service. But the social services did not advise me, just got her away for two days without even asking her. She was 21 at the time. *I now regret that very much.* My daughter cried at night for a long time, bit her fingers and nails, picked the skin off her feet, they must have been sore, but nobody to help. I never saw social services again, only when I went to them for my daughter to have some other company than my own (she then went to the day centre). Maybe this letter will help other parents to try and get support if this happens to them.
>
> (Mrs Alldrich)

> My husband died in his forties, I was 42, and was left with Colin, a mentally handicapped boy aged 11, to look after and two older daughters. That was 15 years ago. If only we'd had a bit more money at the time it would have taken a lot of worries off me. Each and every day I worried, not only about where the next

meal was coming from, but what would become of my son if I should die. Fear was a lead weight around my neck. I didn't know where to turn. No one could give me any advice. With no money in the bank and being unable to work because of Colin it was a hell of a time. But you just have to go on. I have since remarried and I now think if anything happens to us he would miss us dreadfully. He's 26 years old now. We live with the fear that we may die before Colin and worry about what would become of him. He still tears the sheets up, like he did when he was a little boy, and rips off the wallpaper. He cannot cook or clean or take care of himself at all — who's to take care of my gentle giant when I am no longer around?

(Mrs Petersen)

My daughter is approaching 40 and lost her father 8 years ago. He was such a tower of strength. The reaction of my daughter to his death was so bad it naturally makes me wonder what devastation she faces if anything happens to me. This great dread for the future of our handicapped dependants increases as one gets older. Although she has no brothers or sisters she nevertheless has been used to a very caring and loving family life. She likes making hot snacks and drinks, and does little household tasks with me.

(Mrs Dale)

My husband died two years ago. At first my daughter who is mentally handicapped, and was then aged 24, never spoke about his death. And would not attend the funeral. She never accepted the fact she had lost her Dad. After about six months she came with me to visit his grave. She then seemed to accept his death, but I noticed she changed, put on weight for no reason, didn't want to do things she'd liked doing. I also needed advice and help, but never received any. Nobody wanted to know. Now I find she has taken to following me around to know where I am as soon as I leave the room. We have nowhere she could stay around here, she'd have to go miles away if I ever wanted a break. I can't go out in the evenings, even once a month. My other daughters are all grown up now with their own families so they cannot help. I love my daughter and she is a very lovable girl. But just to have somebody to talk to who understands — sometimes I think life is not worth living, but how can I leave her.

(Mrs Yandle)

A widower in his early seventies wrote:

Three months ago my wife died suddenly of a heart attack a few days after her 68th birthday. I decided to meet the minibus bringing our Down's son (Keith aged 30) from the Training Centre and break the news to him before he entered the garden gate and found that his mother was not there to wave to him as usual. His immediate response was to say 'now we are two men together we must look after one another.' He then asked if he could have a framed photograph of his mother and, soon after, if he could sleep in his mother's bed in the room we'd shared. He soon brought in most of his belongings, including a portable TV set and radio recorder, so that, in my 70s, I am very much the junior partner. Keith did not attend his mother's cremation, saying he'd seen one before (his eldest brother's) but he did want to attend an elderly uncle's funeral some six weeks later. He does not often speak of his mother. He teases and plays jokes on me but his health has recently been below par and our doctor thinks that mourning may be a contributory factor.

(Mr Harris)

My husband and Ted had a very close relationship, so much so, that people used to call Ted my husband's shadow. He saw his father suffering a great deal at home before he went into hospital, so I suppose that

was an unhappy time for him, although he never spoke
of it. Of course at this time I was also going through
a very difficult time as I knew my husband was very
ill and about a week before he died, he was told there
was no hope and it was only a matter of time. I sometimes think that he thought I had no feelings over it,
but the fact was I couldn't show my feelings for fear
of letting Ted know the worst. This is how it was when
my husband died, I had to control my feelings. So I
didn't tell Ted his father had died, and the doctor, and
the manager of the centre advised me to let things
drift along for the time being and not say anything.
As time went by I found it was getting more and more
difficult when we met people and they wanted to talk
about my husband, I had to put them off because Ted
was present. Eventually it became such a strain that
I made up my own mind to tell Ted in my own words
about his Dad. Well, when I asked him if he knew
what had happened to his Dad he said 'Yes, my Dad
died!' Unbeknown to me he had been talking about it
to his friends at the Centre. He must have been won-
dering why I hadn't told him or spoken of it.

(Mrs. Vickers)

Mrs Vickers described Ted's disturbed behaviour
during the following months, his withdrawal from her
and his apparent resentment and depression. But her
letter concluded with words of hope:

... lately when I've been out with him he's held my
arm and talked to me again and a couple of times
lately he has got the dominoes and cards out for me to
have a game with him. This he hasn't done for a very
long time, so I'm keeping my fingers crossed. I like to
think that there is a very small light at the end of the
tunnel.

The above letters show some of the dilemmas facing
newly widowed people who are also caring for sons

or daughters with learning difficulties, and the brave manner in which they try to cope with the loneliness and sadness caused by bereavement. During the research work a number of families were met in their own homes, at hostels and hospitals or at meetings of local groups of the Royal Society for Mentally Handicapped Children (MENCAP). The following stories are taken from those meetings, and further illustrate the problems which bereaved families have to face.

Mrs Evans and her daughter Yvonne
Mrs Evans was living in a flat when we met. At the time of her husband's death the family were living in a house in the same town, but within a year of being widowed Mrs Evans moved into a new flat. She said she thought this was a good idea as 'in a new place there would be no sad associations'. Her wish to move house in order to sever sad associations is a common reaction, especially when the dead person has been nursed at home.

Mr and Mrs Evans were in their 50s when he became ill with cancer. Their only daughter Yvonne was then 18. Yvonne had Down's Syndrome, could read, write, and cook, and had spent her adolescence in a residential school. After leaving school she had gone to live in a hostel but spent every other weekend at home. They were a very close and loving family. Mrs Evans said that when her husband became finally very ill and it was obvious that he would only live a few more days she called Yvonne home from the hostel 'so that she could see how very ill he was. She sat by him and understood this'.

Yvonne went back to the hostel before her father died, and was told on the following weekend when she came home again that 'Daddy's gone to heaven'. When the news was broken to her she did not cry at all, and spoke quite contentedly about 'Daddy's gone to heaven'. But on her second visit home after his death, she cried inconsolably and said 'I miss my dad, I miss him sitting there'. In her tears she repeatedly told herself 'he's gone to heaven'. She talked about him a lot to her mother and spoke about the things they all used to do together.

Yvonne was helped to realise the death of her father by having seen him very ill, and at no time was the truth held from her. Her mother's use of the words 'gone to heaven' softened the truth a little, but Yvonne never believed that her father would return. The words 'gone to heaven' were rather a form of comfort, irrespective of her limited intellectual abilities. She used the words to herself as she cried for her father; people with more intellectual ability than Yvonne also use such expressions to comfort themselves. In the early stages of bereavement it is reassuring to envisage the dead person elsewhere, not somewhere accessible and from where they might return one day, such as Australia, but in an acceptable inaccessible spiritual home which is imaginable and safe, although they cannot return from it. By telling herself 'Daddy's gone to heaven' Yvonne was helped to accept the irreversibility of her father's death and the impossibility of his return.

Simplistic traditional Christian concepts of life after death, such as 'going to heaven', which give comfort to some people with learning difficulties may, however, create worries for others. For example, Mrs Dixon said that her daughter Ellen 'could not accept the very final part of death' (the finality of never seeing the person again). She said: 'Ellen used to be very close to her grandmother, who lived round the corner, and she'd go round and help her, and make her tea. When she was poorly she spent a lot of time with her and liked to care for her.' After the grandmother died very suddenly of a heart attack her mother said that Ellen worried a great deal about how she would be looked after in heaven and who would make her tea for her. 'She was very grieved that she would never see her again and worried about who would be talking to her in heaven and caring about her.'

Mrs Sable and her son Frank

Mrs Sable's 28-year-old son, Frank, was a very capable young man with Down's Syndrome, who could read, write, play the piano, cook snacks, and type. His father died in hospital and Frank knew as soon as his mother did, because the hospital staff rang her at 7.00 a.m. to say he was dead and she then told him. He was aware that the death meant he would not see his father again. He also knew what a funeral meant; his mother said that when he was a small child he used to play at funerals with his schoolfriends after having watched Sir Winston Churchill's State funeral on the TV. He went to his father's funeral and now regularly visited the Garden of Remembrance with his mother.

Frank had not developed any difficulties since his mother had been widowed. He had taken on some of the tasks his father once did, such as winding up the clocks and checking that the doors were locked at night. He had been offered a place in a local social services hostel but had turned it down, telling his mother, 'I like keeping you company.' His mother said she was apprehensive about him going to a hostel and 'the dangers of mixing with rough people'.

The sort of worries that Mrs Sable had about Frank leaving home and going to a hostel where there might be 'dangers' (such as lack of supervision, traffic dangers, 'roughness', sexual relationships) are frequently mentioned by parents of people with learning difficulties irrespective of whether the parent is widowed or both partners are still alive and well. These apprehensions are likely to increase in widowhood. There may also be covert wishes to keep the young person at home so as to ease the loneliness of widowhood. As Frank was gentle, thoughtful and not very forceful, it would have been hard for him to assert himself and insist on a life of his own. Such a situation could result in a mother holding on to a son who has learning difficulties, keeping him living at home and restricting his independence.

Mrs Yardley and her daughter Suzie

Thirty-six-year-old Susan Yardley was blind and deaf. Her father died when she was twenty-eight. She was told he had died and afterwards she would sit and say to herself, 'Where's Daddy? Gone to Jesus', as if for reassurance. After her husband's death Mrs Yardley did not receive any help from her family doctor, or a social worker, or the local day care services. She said that she sometimes felt very unwell but never told Suzie 'as she gets nervous of when I'm going to be dead'.

Widows are very careful not to frighten their sons and daughters with the idea that they may one day lose the remaining parent and be all alone. Their wish not to frighten their dependent adult child, and their fears about what will happen if they get ill and die, can make them ignore their own symptoms of illness and avoid seeking medical help. 'I'd be afraid to go to a doctor in case I'd got something wrong. What would happen to her if I had?' said Mrs Yardley.

Mr Nelson and his daughter Mary

Mary Nelson was aged 23. Her intellectual abilities were very limited, and she could do little more than catch a ball, say 'Who are you?' and stir food. When her mother became ill Mary had gone to a hostel for several months, and her mother died in hospital whilst Mary was still in the hostel. She was never told by her family or by the hostel staff that her mother was dead. She had not gone to the funeral as her family said 'she wouldn't understand'.

After she returned home from the hostel her father began to look after her on his own, with prompt arrangements being made by a social worker for him to have a home help, Meals-on-Wheels, and incontinence services and a weekly visit from a district nurse to give Mary a bath. He said he was managing well, as he had a daughter and son living near, and he had a lot of support from them with the washing and regular visits to see if all was well. And his elder daughter came round one evening a week to sit with Mary so that he could go to his club.

'Mary doesn't seem to show any missing of her mother,' said her father. She had not cried for her, nor seemed perturbed at her disappearance. She recognised photos of her, and would also pick out items in a shopping catalogue which reminded her of her mother, such as a handbag and a sewing machine (finding a handbag picture she would say 'Mummy's handbag'). And when the district nurse dressed her after her weekly bath she liked to play the game of 'peepbo' which her mother used to play when dressing her.

It could be thought that Mary's family had underestimated her ability to understand, and her need to have explanations and to know her mother would not return. But they had done what they thought was best for her very limited abilities. They were a caring, loving family, in close contact with each other all the time, and giving Mary much love and security. Their way of coping was to keep the loving family life going on as much as possible in the same way as when the mother was there and not to tell Mary of her death.

Mrs Akroyd and her son Charlie
Charlie Akroyd was 60 years old, and lived at home with his 92-year-old mother. His 96-year-old father had died a year before I met them. Charlie was a very capable person with Down's Syndrome. His parents had believed in integrating him into ordinary education and had sent him to ordinary private and 'council' (LEA) schools, which was very forward-thinking regarding children with learning difficulties in the 1920s and 1930s. His education had ended at 16, after a year in a technical school just before the 1939 War started. He could ride a bike and had enjoyed long cycle rides with his parents during the war years. He had only lived away from his parents for one week, when he went for an assessment in a local day and residential centre at the age of 57.

Charlie's father was ill for six months before he died, and for the last three months he was in hospital and visited daily by Charlie and Mrs Akroyd. Four days before his death he shook Charlie's hand and said, 'Look after your Mum.' The hospital staff telephoned Mrs Akroyd during the night when he died, and she told Charlie when she woke him in the morning. 'He said "Oh, my God" and leapt out of bed,' she said. He had been 'very quiet' since his father's death.

He now went to the day centre three days a week, and the rest of the time he busied himself at home, with his music and books and TV. Mrs Akroyd was receiving help from the local statutory services, more due to the fact that she was very elderly than that she had a son with Down's Syndrome. She had a home help, Meals-on-Wheels, and visits from a local authority social worker. She did not think that she and Charlie were isolated ('we have help, and are comfortable'). She said that she knew Charlie would probably have to go to the residential home in the city when she 'passed on', but she 'didn't think too much about that at the moment.' She was financially secure, with a large and comfortable house, and she felt that this would give Charlie some financial security when he was on his own.

Mrs Kelly and her daughter Joan

Mrs Kelly's 23-year-old daughter Joan was very handicapped. She was unable to feed herself or walk, and her only words were 'Mummy' and 'Hello, Daddy'. When Joan was 21 her 68-year-old father had died after being ill for two years with cancer. Her mother said that Joan had never got used to him being ill and in bed, it had worried her for she had a very close relationship with him ('he was gentle with her and inclined to spoil her').

Seeing a person ill in bed for months before death is dreadfully upsetting, but, in a way, it can also be a preparation for death; a *gradual losing* is experienced and this may be helpful when the person finally dies. However, when there is a very multiply handicapped person to care for in the family and the dying person was one of the carers (as in Joan's family) the disturbance in family routine will cause a feeling of insecurity and this will be made worse because the well parent is suddenly having to care for two members of the family and will be very stressed and over-tired.

Joan began to have residential short-term care as her father worsened. She generally had a few nights away in the local hostel when he went into hospital for his cancer treatment, and this left her mother free to visit him. A handicapped person's first experience of residential care often occurs during a time of emergency or stress at home, and although seeming to be a convenient arrangement at the time, it is likely to cause further insecurity to the family. It must be an intolerable situation for a mother to have a dying husband to care for and to visit in hospital and, at the same time, see a multiply handicapped daughter's care routines getting all upset. The dying parent, too, will be grieved at the handicapped child having to go away. Families who are in this predicament should receive massive support within the home, to try and keep them together, and to keep their own well-tried routines of care for the handicapped child going on as much as possible to avoid extra and unnecessary stress on top of the stress of the terminal illness.

Joan did not go to her father's funeral as it was their family tradition that only men went to funerals. Her mother said: 'After father died she used to keep calling "Daddy, Daddy" all the time; then a few weeks later she did not say "Daddy" any more, but only "Mummy". I've no idea what she thought about her father's death. But when she saw her brother for the first time after Dad died she went mad, wriggled right out of her chair and rolled herself across the floor to him and climbed into his lap calling out with excitement.'

Joan was not usually so attached to her brother, but, as he looked like his father, Mrs Kelly concluded that Joan maybe thought her father had come back. She also reacted like this to an uncle who resembled her father.

Joan's reactions would seem very normal, for great joy *would* be shown if a lost person suddenly returned. Her meetings with her brother and uncle made her think that her father had returned, and she was unable to control her impulsive joy. She also used to watch the front door as if waiting for her father to come home, and would sometimes crawl into his bedroom and stare all around. These reactions would be linked to the normal seeking process that many bereaved persons go through in the initial stages of their loss. It takes time to fully realise a loss and it is normal to want to search a while as if partly believing that the dead person will be found again and partly because there is a need to confirm that they really have gone and will not be found again (see also Chapter 1).

Mrs Kelly said that after her bereavement she had not received any support from health services or the social services department and no community nurse or social worker had ever called to see how she was managing. During the first year following her husband's death she decided that Joan should go to a private hostel some 20 miles away, thinking that if she was happy there she could stay permanently and come home for weekends. The idea was that Joan would be already settled in a home in the event of Mrs Kelly dying. She initially went for one month, but stayed for five, coming home every weekend.

However, Joan deteriorated at the hostel. Understandably, she could not cope with the additional losses of her home and mother and home routines so soon after losing her father. Her mother said, 'She went down. She was very upset, grief-stricken, and got all withdrawn. She began to cry non-stop and the manager of the hostel called a doctor out to her and

she was sedated.' After five months there Joan seemed
so upset that her mother brought her home for good.

After her return home Joan then received occasional
short-term care at a residential unit run jointly by
the local social services department and a charitable
organisation, but her mother was depressed about a)
the lack of promise to help in an emergency and b)
having no official help from anyone in planning a
secure future for Joan.

Sometimes Mrs Kelly felt like a prisoner in the
house as she could not drive and her husband's car
had been sold after he died. It was very difficult for
her to take Joan out in her wheelchair because it
was heavy to push and Mrs Kelly was in poor health
because of gynaecological problems and overweight.
She felt constantly low and unwell in a depressed way,
feeling abandoned and as if nobody cared; she said,
'I've had no visit from a social worker for two years . . .
I feel absolutely alone . . . I've given up all activities
since my husband died, my Women's Institute meetings and evening classes, as there's nobody to sit with
Joan . . . I'm haunted too, by the idea of my dying and
her going to the big mental handicap hospital . . .'

The loneliness which is felt after a bereavement,
combined with the isolation which the majority of middle-aged and elderly parents of handicapped sons and
daughters have to cope with anyway, can be almost
intolerable. 'Dad took a lot of responsibility for Joan —
we shared all her routines, dressing and feeding her
together, and bathing her, and then having our hot
drinks together before going to bed. We used to go
out on drives together. Now, there's nothing to look
forward to.'

The loving routines, so poignantly remembered, so
much part of their shared and sheltered life, all three

of them together, had now become a depressing chore
for the mother left alone to care for her very dependent
daughter.

Mrs Hill and her son Ian

Ian Hill was 22 years old when his father died suddenly in the middle of the night, of a heart attack. His
mother said she would have liked to tell him gently
about the death, but he was woken up by hearing the
ambulance men and police in the hall and began to
scream. She told him, 'Dad's gone to Jesus and one
day we shall see him again.' It was unfortunate that
Ian had to learn about his father's death in the middle
of the night amongst the excitement of ambulance men
and policemen in the house. His mother's words 'gone
to Jesus' were meant to be a gentle, reassuring explanation of what had happened, but under the dramatic
circumstances must have made him think that going
to Jesus was a very frightening event.

Ian did not go to the funeral but he was shown all
the flowers, and his sister stayed at home with him
whilst the other members of the family went. 'Afterwards, in the following months, he used to watch the
door, waiting for his Dad to come back', said his
mother. Five years later he experienced another death
in the family and had the same reaction as when his
father had died — screams, sobs, loss of appetite and
loss of weight.

Ian was just as handicapped as Joan Kelly, being
physically immobile and with very limited speech, but
his initial reactions in the first few weeks following
his father's death were more panic-stricken and violent than Joan's reactions had been. Perhaps this was
because he had less preparation than Joan, for the
death of his father occurred very suddenly and was

complicated by the dramatic arrival of the police and ambulance men. Joan's worst reactions had occurred a few months later when she went away into residential care, suggesting that her additional losses of home, mother and home routines were too much for her.

Mrs Tamas and her daughter Queenie

In middle-aged and elderly families there are likely to be several deaths within a short period of time, making people feel that life is a continuous experience of death. Twenty-six-year-old Queenie, a multiply handicapped woman who was living at home with her parents, experienced in one year the death of her father and two grandparents and an uncle who had been a very close member of the family. Queenie was partially sighted, with hearing losses and an unsteady walk. The deaths of these four much-loved people took away all her confidence. She lost her ability to dress herself and was unable to walk for several weeks. When she did begin to walk again she clung tightly to her mother's arm all the time, and if they went shopping her mother had difficulty in disentangling Queenie's hands from her arm, whereas previously she had enjoyed walking round the supermarket with her hands on the trolley.

Queenie became very distressed when her mother had a hospital appointment about fifteen months after the bereavements had occurred. She overheard her talking to a neighbour about going to the hospital, and asked her if she was going away and going to die like father and the grandparents and Uncle Sam. Queenie's mother, being physically not very well herself and still suffering from the grief of the multiple losses, had little reserve of physical or emotional energy to help

Queenie with the problems that the bereavements had caused.

* * *

Five particular issues emerged from the family letters and meetings:

* The problem of how to break the news of a death to a person with learning difficulties;
* Widows fantasising about the death not having occurred;
* The fears of widows concerning their own deaths, and the fears of sons and daughters with learning difficulties that their remaining parent will die;
* Widows and their sons or daughters with learning difficulties trapping each other;
* Loneliness, and the need for help after a bereavement.

The following discussion considers these five issues.

The problem of how to break the news of a death to a person with learning difficulties

One of the most distressing problems for parents or relatives, friends or professionals is how to tell a person with a learning difficulty that somebody close to them has died. Breaking bad news is always very stressful, and the teller has some degree of expectation that the recipient will support them by making appropriate remarks of understanding. If the person being told is very multiply handicapped and also has a speech or hearing disability, the person breaking the news may not only worry about how much is understood, but also be upset on his or her own account in case the handicapped person makes inappropriate remarks or gets emotionally out of control, or can only remain completely silent.

The interviewed widows were asked if they had any advice to give to other parents about how to break the news of a death to their sons or daughters; one mother said, 'No, I can give no advice, I had no idea what words to use to explain it to my son.' Her reply was typical of the replies received and showed the stress and emotional confusion that some bereaved parents have regarding this issue.

Some of the parents met during the research said that they should definitely have received more professional help in breaking the news. They found particular difficulties in knowing what words to use, whether to let them see the dead person, whether to let them see adults crying, whether to let them go to the funeral. A few of the parents, who had a close relationship with a known social worker, had asked them to break the news. It was surprising to find that some professionals (family doctors, teachers, social workers, nurses) had advised parents not to disclose immediately that the death had occurred but to wait a while before breaking the news. But they had not been specific about how long to wait and had not followed up their advice. This meant that parents might put off breaking the news for many months.

The wide difference in the abilities of people with learning difficulties makes it impossible to give firm advice about how to break the news of a death. Some will be as capable as anybody else of understanding what has happened, but others do find it confusing to have somebody they love suddenly disappearing out of their lives. Their confusion is not helped, however, if the other members of the family act secretively or strangely, or tell stories about where the person has gone, or cry in other rooms.

Some families are completely honest right from the beginning, even when the death is shocking because of being unexpected. For example: Winnie Pringle was 35 years old when her 72-year-old father was instantly killed in a road accident. Her mother had died when Winnie was seven years old and she had always lived at home with her father and brothers and sisters. The news of her father's fatal accident was given to her by her brother-in-law, who had a close relationship with her. Her immediate reaction was to cry a lot, and her first words were, 'Did he say anything?' Her brother-in-law replied that her father had said, 'Look after Winnie'. He thought this remark would give her security and comfort and was in keeping with what her father would have wanted her to be told. It was a very kind 'white lie', for it affirmed Winnie's continuing security and gave a reassurance that she would be cared for by the remaining members of the family. When her father's body was brought to the house she helped to carry in the coffin and place it in the big downstairs room. After she had done this she said, 'Right, he's home now.' She was not excluded from the funeral and she regularly visits his grave with other members of her family.

It would seem that if widowed parents keep bad news from a person with learning difficulties it is because they are themselves too distressed to explain it, rather than believing that the person does not merit normal consideration and honesty. From a mixture of kindness and their own distress they think they will save the son or daughter from unnecessary anguish by not telling them the truth. So a story may be told to explain the disappearance of the person who has died. If the truth is not told from the start it is possible that a train of imaginative stories will get going in the months following the death, and these may lead to fantasies which the widow, in grief and emotional distress, will herself collude with and from which she may even begin to derive some comfort.

Widows fantasising about the death not having occurred

After a person has died it is understandable if the surviving member of the family who was most close to them lives for a while in a state of half-belief, wanting still to do the things that they did when that person was alive. Some bereaved people find it very hard to clear out the dead person's belongings and clothes. Favourite items of clothing may be kept for a very long time. One widow said, 'I've not got rid of his best suit, and funnily enough I've still left his hankie in the pocket, although I know he'll never use it again.' It is very hard to let go of everything at once: the shared habits, thoughts, phrases, conversations and details of life-style are woven into one's own identity and existence. One of the difficult aspects of bereavement is the shared identity which the dead person takes with them, so the person left behind feels as if a part of them too has gone into obscurity.

The bereaved person may even have moments of pretending that the death has not occurred: they may look out of the window to see the person come home; may say 'good night' when putting out the light; may even call quietly 'I'm home' when opening the front door after returning from shopping. Repeating again some of the shared habits and words, tentatively, whispering and in private, is not abnormal and may even be helpful as an aid to gradually letting go, helping them to accept the full realisation that the dead person has really gone for good and to accept that the words of greeting, and glances from the window, are needed no more. Momentarily fantasising that the dead person is still there, one gets a reassurance that they did indeed once exist and were once part of one's own life-style.

Such fantasies will pass after serving the purpose of being an initial and very private help; friends and relatives will probably never know about them. However, if there is a person living at home who has severe difficulties in verbal understanding, a widow may be encouraged to act out the fantasies over a long period. Some widows looking after very dependent sons and daughters maintain elaborate fantasies over a long time: pretending that the person is still alive, in hospital or on holiday, or gone on a journey. After a while the fantasy which started because they could not bear to explain what has really happened may become an extension of their own disbelief about the death.

Prolonged fantasies are likely to occur if the widow is living a socially isolated life with her dependent son or daughter and has also been advised by professionals that he or she should not be told what has happened. Fiona Isaacs was nineteen years old when her elderly father died in hospital after a long illness. She was the youngest of the family and the others were all married and gone from the home. The family doctor advised Fiona's mother not to tell her about the father's death because he thought that she would get 'very upset and add to the problems'. So Fiona's mother told her 'Dad has gone away to another hospital and this is too far away to visit.' Fiona believed this story and remained her usual cheery self. Her mother was meanwhile mourning her dead husband and trying to adapt to her widowhood. She found it very painful to maintain the falsehood, because Fiona talked continuously about going to visit her father in the 'new hospital' and when her mother said that this was not possible she began to write letters and make little presents to send him. At times her mother found that maintaining all this make-believe with Fiona was unbearable, but sometimes she found herself going along with the pretence almost contentedly and she recognised how easy it would be to fall into a fantasy of pretending that her husband was not dead.

For several years one widow regularly helped her daughter to write a letter to her dead husband and every Sunday afternoon they would walk together to the letter box and post it, the mother pretending it was going to him in a hospital a long way off. Another widow, whose husband had been killed by an attack in Ireland, pretended for three months that he was on a course; and another, whose husband had once been a long-distance lorry driver, pretended that he had gone on a very long journey with his lorry.

Another widow elaborated a story of the dead father being on a long journey and she gave her son intricate details and descriptions of where the father was each week. Another promised her daughter 'He'll come back one day'. Loneliness, social isolation, lack of professional support, will encourage such extended fantasies.

Situations like these are likely to occur when professionals fail to recognise that people with learning difficulties need to know the truth, even if it is painful. Professionals often say that the truth will make the person create more problems for the widow, but there is little evidence to support this theory. However, if 'more problems' do occur, additional professional support should be made available throughout that time. It is not good enough for professionals just to say 'don't tell them or you'll add to your problems' and then disappear off the scene, and leave the widow and her child pretending that the death has not happened.

Sometimes, however, the cause of fantasising cannot be attributed entirely to the poor ability of the person with a learning difficulty nor to any unwise advice given by professionals, but will develop because of the pain and distress caused by a very sad and difficult-to-accept death, such as that of a much loved husband; or because the death has been unexpected or untimely, and there has been none of the preparation which a long illness might give. In these extra painful circumstances the bereaved person may react in a manner which is not in character and not as they reacted to previous bereavements (see Chapter 4, the story of Peggy Benchly, pages 118–22.

The fears of widows concerning their own deaths, and the fears of the sons and daughters with learning difficulties that their remaining parent will die

A death in the family brings an increased awareness of one's own mortality and this is frightening to think about when there is a dependent person to care for at home. The person suddenly seems very vulnerable indeed when there is only one parent left to look after them. The widowed parent then has heart-rending worries about 'what will happen to him when I'm gone too?' They may develop fears about their own health, and some widows have a terrible nightmare image about dying and not being found for several days and the handicapped person being helpless in the house, hungry and neglected or in danger from the gas or electricity.

In the early 1980s a group of older parents living in Harrow Weald (London) and belonging to the local MENCAP Group gave each other written details of what should be done in the event of their own sudden deaths; these contained addresses, phone numbers of relatives and friends, and notes about their son's and daughters' likes, dislikes and abilities. The parents felt a sense of relief at having made these plans.

At the parent meetings attended during this study there was always anxious discussion about the practical issues which would arise following both parents' deaths, for examples where the son or daughter would live and the quality of their physical care. There was, however, a reluctance to discuss the likelihood of them suffering grief at the death of their parents. This was usually too distressing to think about or to discuss. The mother of a school age child said, 'I've always been worried about what will happen to Nigel when we are both dead, but I've never before thought about who would help him if he was grief-stricken — his grief at our dying had not occurred to me. I cannot bear to think of it.'

Nevertheless it is obvious that people with learning difficulties will grieve at the deaths of parents, relatives, and friends, and in the months following a loss they will worry about the likelihood of further losses. Mr Higgins, widowed in his later fifties and left looking after a 21-year-old daughter with Down's Syndrome, said that in the first year after his wife's death his daughter would often come into his bedroom at night and he would wake up to find her standing there in her dressing-gown and saying, 'You still here, Dad? You've not gone?' (See also Queenie, pages 56–7.)

Widows and their sons and daughters trapping each other

In the trauma of their bereavement newly widowed parents and their sons or daughters who have learning difficulties may develop a life-style which begins well and is initially very helpful and creates a sense of security for them, but eventually traps them. A fear of loneliness and an inability to make any effort to develop a life outside the home, combined with a wish to protect the son or daughter from what might be considered 'outside dangers', may result in a widow holding on to the young person and preventing them from having an independent life of their own.

Some people with learning difficulties may fall into the role of being 'captive companions'. For example, Bert was in his late twenties and was keen to go and live with a group of friends in a hostel, but his mother was adamant that he should not leave home. 'He's happy here, why go to a hostel?' she said. She had been widowed for four years, and since then she and her son had settled into a routine of evenings at home together which she would obviously miss if he left home. He was very amiable about his mother's wish to keep him at home and it seemed that his good nature and lack of experience in asserting himself at home was stopping him from having an independent adult life.

In another family there was a similarly capable son with Down's syndrome, and he decided after his father died that he was 'now the man of the house.' He took over the jobs that his father had once done. This was initially very helpful, but he gradually became very bossy and objectionable and his mother seemed to need some outside professional help to encourage him to leave home.

Loneliness and the need for help after a bereavement

All the widows who were contacted said that they felt lonely. The loneliness was worse when the handicapped son or daughter was very physically disabled and the married couple had shared all the care routines.

'We used to do everything together,' said the widowed mother of a totally helpless 22-year-old daughter. 'When we woke up in the morning my husband would bang on the wall beside the bed to her and say "We're awake" and we'd hear her give her special cry out to let us know that she had heard. And all day we'd be busy together, right up to our night-time drink together. I'd make the cocoa and he'd sit by the fire with her on his lap watching the 10 o'clock news on the TV.'

Her poignant description of their long-shared routines expressed the sad loneliness experienced by widows left caring single-handed for multiply handicapped sons and daughters. With her husband's death this widow had lost not only her much loved husband and all his companionship and love, but also a partner in caring for their very dependent daughter. The lives of the couple had been isolated for a very long time, due to their child being so helpless and needing such a lot of care, but they had not complained about the constrictions that her needs caused and they had worked out good routines together. The husband's death completely shattered the secure routines that the care of their daughter demanded, not only within the home but outside as well; there would be no more drives out in the car or walking round the park together at weekends. There was an intolerable emptiness left, and a need for physical help that was not being met by the statutory services.

Sometimes the loneliness was made worse because the few friends that the married couple did have dropped away after the husband's death, and even other members of the family did not visit so often. So if the son or daughter was multiply handicapped and difficult to get out, this could mean very severe isolation for the new widow. The widowed mother of a severely multiply handicapped daughter, said: 'Worst of all, my own son gradually stopped coming round after Dad died. I don't know if it was because he couldn't bear seeing us without Dad here or because he didn't know what to talk about to me. He worked at the same firm as Dad was in before he retired and they used to gossip together for hours about the firm and what was going on there now. My daughter and I liked to listen and hear them laugh. But my son doesn't come round so much now, and we miss all that chatting. My daughter cannot speak at all.'

It is possible that the isolation experienced by younger widows — those in their fifties or sixties — may be worse than for those in their eighties. It is an effort for any newly widowed middle-aged person to make a new 'social life' for themselves, even in a very modest way such as going to an evening class, but if the widow has the full-time care of a very dependent son or daughter it is impossible for him or her to build up any social life at all unless there is well-organised help available. But that help needs to be appropriate for the mentally handicapped person and not demeaning for them, for example they should not be placed in unsuitable institutions for short periods; this often happens, and can be described as little more than 'kennelling' and may well have detrimental effects (Oswin, 1984[1]).

From what was said by the families it would seem that some widows in their eighties and nineties are not so isolated as the younger ones with regard to getting helpful local services, because the fact of being elderly had already linked them to services for elderly people, such as home helps, chiropody, Meals-on-Wheels, and district nurses (see Mrs Akroyd, pages 50 and 51). These professional contacts serve as a form of 'social life', whereas widows in their fifties or sixties, who are managing their son's or daughter's care very expertly on their own, sometimes do not see anybody from one week's end to another.

If the parents were long-term members of a voluntary organisation connected with their child's handicap (MENCAP, Down's Syndrome Association, Spastics Society) there might be less loneliness after a death. Older parents belonging to MENCAP local groups try to support each other (see page 64). Many of them have known one another for over twenty-five years, and have been helpful at various times of crisis. But these contemporaries, getting elderly themselves and perhaps already widowed and with handicapped adult sons and daughters at home, cannot always give each other much more support than a phone call for a chat, or arrange a lift to monthly meetings, although there is much sympathy and understanding of each other's problems ('we're all in the same boat, on our own' — 'we're worried about the future and not confident about the services we are getting').

When a family threesome — mother, father and very dependent adult son or daughter — has been coping well and not making any demands on local services, they may not be known by any of the local professionals, such as the GP, district nursing services, social workers, or community mental handicap nurses. This can mean that when a sudden bereavement occurs the widow will be without support and have to start searching for help as the problems build up. She may have little or no knowledge or experience of the available services to which she is entitled. Searching for help is not only difficult but depressing, especially when the widow and child are already low with their feelings of loss and grief. It is hard to seek help at the best of times, and worse when one is sad and tired. Widows might be less at risk to depression if there had been forward planning by their local authorities, so that they could be promptly linked to appropriate services.

The amount of help obtainable may be connected with the way in which the person died: for example, if there has been a long illness and the dying person has been nursed at home with the help of district nurses, the family are more likely to receive prompt help because they are already known by the local professionals. But if the death is very sudden and the family not known then they tend to go into a sad obscurity.

Sometimes the degree of help available depends on the sex of the widowed person; fathers left caring for handicapped sons or daughters seem to get help more readily than mothers do, probably because it is believed that a man left on his own is not likely to manage competently the domestic affairs of the house and the care of a severely handicapped person. For example, Mr Nelson (pages 49–50) was promptly linked to district help, such as home help, Meals-on-Wheels and incontinence services. Another father who was left alone caring for a very dependent daughter was immediately offered Meals-on-Wheels because it was believed that as he was a man he would not be able to cook (in fact he was a master baker and had done most of the family cooking for many years).

Differences in attitude and services available according to the sex of the widowed carer and the person requiring the personal care seemed also to be linked with sexual propriety and what was considered to be appropriate or 'right' for a father to do. For example, bathing a helpless adult daughter was not considered 'right' for a father to do, so help was promptly arranged; whereas few eyebrows were raised at a widowed mother bathing a helpless adult son.

Many of the widows felt aggrieved that their local social services departments and health authorities had 'not been near' since the bereavement had occurred. It was indeed remarkable to find, in the areas visited, that there was no firm forward planning to help the parents of sons and daughters who had learning difficulties, in times of bereavement: there was no promise that appropriate day services and transport would be readily available, and the local community services were not promptly arranged to help with the tasks once done with the deceased partner, such as bathing a very handicapped young adult.

The worries, grief and loneliness of the widows and their sons and daughters cannot be entirely prevented, but they could be eased by timely and appropriately planned services.

REFERENCE

1   Oswin, M. *They Keep Going Away* (King Edward's Hospital Fund for London, London, 1984).

3 BEREAVED PEOPLE IN RESIDENTIAL CARE

> We cried together. It was sad, I didn't care. The nursing officer came in and saw me crying and seemed to think I had got too emotionally involved, but why should I be ashamed of my tears?
>
> Sister of a ward in a mental handicap hospital

Changes in attitudes towards mentally handicapped people over the last decade and the welcome closure of the big old institutions has meant that many people with moderate or severe learning difficulties are now living fairly independently in ordinary housing; for example, two or three friends will be together in a house or flat and look after themselves with appropriate help given by local health or social services as necessary; or a small group of more severely handicapped people will live in a staffed house. Varieties of residential care are run by local authority social service departments, local health authorities, housing associations and voluntary organisations. However, this chapter refers only to bereaved mentally handicapped people who were still living in the large, more traditional hospitals and hostels at the time of the research.

PART ONE: TRADITIONS IN RESIDENTIAL CARE

Long-term care

Until well into the 1970s the care in some of the long-stay institutions was often rigid and restrictive, or even shamefully neglectful (Ockendon[1] and Ely[2] Reports), and the more sensitive and forward-looking staff had an uphill battle to achieve any improvements for the residents.

Admittance to a long-stay institution in childhood was common in England until the 1980s (and still continues in Scotland). Many of the people who are still in the large mental handicap hospitals have been hospitalised for thirty or forty years. Admitting a child to a long-stay hospital often caused loss of family contact because visiting was not very easy for parents. Many of the hospitals were situated a long distance away, isolated in the countryside, with little public transport to them; sometimes the visiting rules were restricted to certain days and hours, and sometimes the parents were made to feel that their visits upset their children and held back their progress. In some hospitals, even as late as the 1970s, the visiting took place publicly in a large hall in the hospital, like prison visiting.

Gabriel Oak's experiences were not unusual. He had been admitted to a long-stay hospital in the 1930s, when he was seven years old. He had been assessed by his local public health department as 'a medium grade imbecile'. From the age of seven he had to work continuously at the task of weaving face flannels and dishcloths, and when he was eight years old he was criticised in his medical notes as 'no good, unable to make face flannels'. By the age of eleven his notes described him as 'making some progress in making face flannels'. He lived in the hospital for forty-six years. In 1982 he was transferred to a twenty-bedded hostel run by the local health authority.

Forty-year-old Barry Brown was admitted to a mental handicap hospital in South London at the age of three. He lived there for seventeen years and was then sent to another hospital where he stayed until he was 31. His parents then asked for his transfer to the North East because they had retired there. After spending eight years in a big traditional hospital in Yorkshire he was sent to a smaller unit. This final placement was considered best for him as it was near his family. Barry had spent thirty-six years in large, remote institutions but his parents had managed to keep good contact with him.

The bad effects of institutional care on the development of young children has been well-documented (Bowlby, 1951;[3] Robertson 1958;[4] Tizard, King and Raynes 1971;[5] Oswin, 1971,[6] 1978,[7] 1984[8]); however, the professionals coming into contact with Barry in his adulthood seemed singularly unaware of his deprived childhood and were more ready to blame his parents for his undeveloped potential than the institution in which he grew up. In 1980 a doctor wrote about the Brown family: 'The family are nice but it seems that he has been over-protected and over-indulged to some extent over the years and this may have restricted his potential somewhat.'

Even in the small unit to which Barry was transferred in order to be near his family, where one would have thought that attitudes to families would be more positive, the staff still failed to respect the family ties. Barry's mother became very ill soon after his move to the small unit, but the staff decided they should not tell him because they were very worried about 'the trouble he's going to cause if his mum dies'. Staff caring for anybody in Barry's situation would need to be sensitive to his insecurities, disappointments and grief, but they made no plans to prepare him for a loss and to support him through grief. His move to the local unit had been centred on 'being near mum', but the closer contact was finishing almost before it had begun. Life for Barry must have seemed one huge broken promise of happiness.

The closure of the large hospitals and the move of people with learning difficulties out to small homes in the community has generally meant closer family contact, but for some people, as in Barry's case, the moves from hospital to community has coincided with the beginning of their parents' terminal illness or frailty and death. So, whilst trying to settle into their new homes where they thought that they would be near their parents and seeing a lot of them, they have found they were in the process of losing them. Their moves out, having taken many years to effect, were sadly too late.

Short-term residential care
Short-term residential care, like long-term care, has been traditionally one of the services organised for people with handicaps, for example a few weeks of residential care in a hospital or home is sometimes arranged if a person with a learning difficulty is living at home and a parent becomes ill. Professionals may believe that short-term care is a very good service but handicapped people and their families often associate it with feelings of anxiety and insecurity because it is not planned in a manner which suits the individual concerned. A first experience of residential care, even

if only lasting for a few days or a week or two, can be a bad experience of loss for a person who has never left home before. Mentally handicapped children taken into short-term care as a means of giving parents relief are known to suffer considerable home-sickness (Oswin, 1984[8]), and there is no reason to suppose that adults do not suffer equal homesickness. Indeed, it would seem that admittance to any form of residential care, at any age and for whatever reason (family illness, family rest, the assessment or education of the handicapped person) is an experience of loss and will provoke feeling of grief.

If a parent dies whilst a person with learning difficulties is in short-term care he or she may stay permanently in the hospital or hostel and never go home again, although they had expected to return home after a few days and had been promised that they would 'soon see mum again, she'll be better soon', perhaps even being told 'if you are good you'll soon see mum again and go home'.

The following three stories illustrate how short-term care is used and also how it may very easily become long-term care.

Abdou was having short-term care in a local authority hostel, because his mother had had to go into hospital for an operation. He was very worried and upset. His father had died a few years earlier after going into hospital for an operation. As Abdou's previous experience of having a parent in hospital was the death of that parent, he probably thought that he would never see his mother again, so it was no wonder he was upset. Having short-term residential care at such a stressful time greatly increased his anxieties. He might have felt more secure and in control of his situation if he could have remained in his own home with a relative, or neighbour, friend or professional staying with him.

Short-term care becomes long-term care in circumstances where the parents are elderly and ill. For example 62-year-old *Violet Cobbet* had always lived at home with her parents. When her 85-year-old mother went into hospital for an operation Violet had short-term residential care in a local home for people with learning difficulties because her father was in his nineties and could not look after her on his own. Violet and her parents expected her to stay in the home for just a few weeks, but her mother died in the hospital after the operation, and Violet never went home again. Her father died a year later. She had never been separated from her parents, nor been away from home, then within two years she lost both parents and her home. The immensity of her losses must have been very shocking. The staff commented, 'Violet went to her parents' funerals, but did not seem to be affected.'

The following story, of *Bridget Reed*, casts doubts on whether she should have been in short-term care in the first place, and poses the question: what is the point of causing disturbances in families which are managing very well and have not requested changes to be made? Bridget was born in 1944 and had Down's Syndrome. She had apparently been a very lively and forthright little girl, but although very capable and fairly independent, she never went to school. When she was five years old she had been given an assessment of her abilities (the doctor who assessed her wrote in her notes, 'she made numerous defiant gestures during the interview'). During her childhood and early adolescence she was sent to various centres, at that time called 'occupation centres', because mentally handicapped children were not eligible for education under local education authorities until the 1970 Education (Handicapped Children) Act. At the age of 14 she left the occupation centre and stayed at home, and there was no further contact with any local social service departments or health authorities until her mother died in 1971, when Bridget was twenty-seven years old. Her father was then seventy-two, but the two of them coped well, cooking, doing the household chores together and generally helping each other. But four years later a report from a visiting social worker who had heard about them through the local MENCAP group referred rather disapprovingly to her living with her 76-year-old father and said that 'he was anxious about what would happen to Bridget if he died'.

It was decided that the only solution to her father's anxieties about the future was to admit Bridget to a large institution some forty miles from her home. She had two periods of short-term care there in 1975 and three in 1976. It was too far away for her aged father to visit her. In 1977 she was admitted there permanently, but returned to her home town seven years later when the hospitals began to close down and she got a place in a local hostel within easy reach of her father. He was then aged 84, but still fit. He was very pleased that his daughter had returned to live near him.

*   *   *

The foregoing references to traditions in residential care suggest that many middle-aged and elderly people with learning difficulties have a long history of institutionalisation with accompanying bad experiences of loss and separation in childhood simply because at that time all services for mentally handicapped people were organised on the basis of family separation and institutionalisation. What happened to Gabriel Oak and Barry Brown also happened to thousands of others. Nobody can say with certainty how those early experiences of loss may affect the reactions of adults with learning difficulties when they suffer a bereavement, but their childhood experience should be borne in mind when a bereavement occurs, for any fresh loss may reactivate the grief and anxieties which were felt in earlier losses.

PART TWO: WHO IS RESPONSIBLE FOR BEING SENSITIVE?

The residential care facilities which were visited during the research, whether large hospitals or smaller community units, showed a mixture of good and bad practices regarding how the nurses and care staff and other professionals coped with the problems of bereavement amongst the residents. There appear to be several reasons behind bad practices; for example, professionals often stereotype people with learning difficulties and think of them as children who need protection from the realities of life, or as people whose emotions do not exist or should not be encouraged. Care staff and nurses are also inclined to give more priority to controlling likely behaviour problems and keeping the hospital or hostel running quietly than to helping a bereaved person.

Sometimes bad practices occur because staff do not have any knowledge of the emotional pain that may be caused by a death and the variety of ways in which people will express their grief. Or, staff may recognise the pain caused by a bereavement but find the subject of death so personally painful that they avoid discussing it or even acknowledging it and become accustomed to denying their own and other people's feelings of upset and tenderness.

The following discussion considers some of these complicated issues and how they can have a negative influence on the organisation of care and support for bereaved people in residential units.

Immediate admission to residential care

Professionals sometimes panic and make hasty decisions when a death occurs in a family where there is a person with a learning difficulty. Panic decisions may make a social worker, district nurse, community nurse or family doctor arrange an immediate admission to residential care. The person then experiences a sudden loss of everyone and everything that is familiar: the parent who has just died, the home environment and routines, personal possessions, pets, neighbourhood and friends, their familiar bed and sometimes even their own clothes — all are suddenly gone and they are expected to settle down in a new environment with strangers. Such an experience would be a likely cause of breakdown for anybody, let alone a person who may already be disadvantaged by severe physical handicaps and learning difficulties and who may have led a very sheltered life at home with caring parents.

People who have always lived at home are likely to find difficulty in understanding the rules of mass living, and may well feel that they have entered a very alien world. Institutional rules may exclude them from their bedrooms during the day and from the kitchen at all times, even if when they were at home with their parents they had been quite independent and helped with the housework and cooking or had spent a lot of time sitting in the kitchen whilst their parents cooked and washed up.

It would seem that mentally handicapped people's roles within their family home may be under-estimated by professionals. Thirty-nine-year-old Muriel Johns lived at home with her widowed mother and was used to helping her and doing the housework and cooking. When her mother suddenly died Muriel was removed from the home within an hour and immediately admitted to a hospital many miles away, where she arrived grief-stricken and shocked. Her grief was made worse because she was also worried about the house; being the only surviving member of her family she felt some responsibility for it.

The plight of people with *multiple handicaps*, those who may be blind, cerebral palsied, speechless and non-ambulant in addition to having learning difficulties, is particularly poignant when their caring parents die. It is an enormous physical and emotional shock for these very dependent and physically helpless people to enter a new environment. Their settling-in to residential care poses immense problems because the care staff cannot reproduce exactly the familiar security that the bereaved person was accustomed to at home.

Familiar security would have been in the routines of care their parents gave them: in the way they were helped to eat and drink; their clothes, the lights, smells, and sounds of the house, foods and drinks, cups and spoons, ways of being lifted, held and touched, of being washed, dressed and talked to. All this suddenly disappears when they are admitted to residential care and it is understandable if they suffer intense grief. Sometimes the bereaved person will develop an illness which may be linked with severe grief and pining — for example, digestive disorders, headaches, loss of weight. They may show their grief by a failure to eat and drink. Some of the staff who were met during the research visits to institutions expressed worries over the possibility of extreme pining and even death amongst very dependent newly admitted bereaved persons. The staff in one health service hostel referred to three middle-aged residents who were admitted after their parents died and who all died themselves of heart attacks within twelve months.

Perhaps it is difficult for a professional who is suddenly faced with a bereaved and very dependent person to realise that they need continuing love and security just as much as they need a new roof over their heads and a new set of people to look after their physical needs; but instead of being immediately admitted to an institution without any appropriate explanation and preparation it would be more helpful for bereaved persons to remain in their own homes with a professional or volunteer or friend staying with them for a few weeks until other, calmer, arrangements could be made. In this way they could be included in plans and introduced slowly to their new home.

The near-panic of professionals faced with a situation with which they are unfamiliar can result in very inappropriate, even bizarre, arrangements being made. During a meeting which was held to discuss the problems of bereaved people an incidence was described of a man with Down's Syndrome who had to stay overnight, sitting on a bench, in the out-patient department of a large district general hospital after his widowed mother had suddenly died at home. The people who had come to the house after her death had not met him before and had never worked with people with learning difficulties and they made this panic arrangement without any thought for his needs.

Multiple moves

When grieving for somebody who has recently died it is sometimes very hard to tolerate any further form of loss or change, even if only temporary; one feels a need for life to continue in a familiar fashion as much as possible as it was before the death occurred; it is as if a saturation point can be reached with grief and no more can be tolerated. So a move to a new neighbourhood, or a close friend going away on holiday, or changes of staff if one is living in residential care, may provoke feelings of grief which may not seem commensurate with the nature of that loss or change. Thus it is unwise for too many changes to be made in the lives of people with learning difficulties when they lose a parent.

However, some professionals augment people's grief by increasing their losses at critical times. For instance, many mentally handicapped persons have a disturbing number of residential care placements during the months after the death of the parent or other person with whom they have been living. First they may have an 'emergency' or 'crisis' admission for the first few nights after the death; this temporary stay may be in a local authority short-term hostel, a mental handicap hospital, or even in the ward of a general or geriatric hospital. They will then be moved on to another temporary residential placement for an 'assessment'. After two or three months in the assessment unit they will be moved on to their third placement, which is expected to be their permanent home. The decision about this final placement will be based on how they showed up in tests of competence and skills at the assessment centre. However, the third placement sometimes breaks down because the person finds it hard to settle, and they may then be re-admitted back into the assessment unit and the search for a permanent placement will start all over again. Some people with learning difficulties have as many as five different residential care placements during the first year after a bereavement.

Experiencing so many changes immediately after a major bereavement understandably results in their becoming very disturbed and unhappy. Oliver Austin was in his twenties when his 54-year-old widowed mother suddenly died. As an emergency he was admitted to a social services hostel where he stayed for a week. He was next moved to an 'assessment house' run by the local health authority. The intention was that he should be assessed for his competence in household tasks and looking after himself. After he had been there for three months the assessment panel decided that he could go back to the social services hostel as he would fit in there as a permanent resident. But when he arrived back there his behaviour became difficult and he began to get described in his notes as 'disturbed', and was quite soon rejected by the hostel staff and moved on yet again, this time to a home for people with behaviour problems. He arrived there with the label of being 'difficult and disturbed'. The staff at this fourth placement noted that he was 'anxious and depressed'.

Oliver's upset behaviour was understandable and normal, for he had been subjected to constant upheavals, stress and insecurity ever since his mother's death twelve months earlier: extraordinary demands had been made on him to settle calmly in to various new homes, to make successful relationships with a large number of strangers, and to fulfil a battery of rigorous assessment tests.

Behaviour which would be considered normal for a bereaved person who has *not* got a learning difficulty is often labelled 'difficult' when occurring with a person who has (see also Chapter 1). Tears, depression, tempers and irritability are normal responses to bereavement *and* to being constantly moved about to a series of residential placements, but the label 'difficult' will be used because the staff do not appreciate the unsettling effects of too many moves on top of a bereavement. Also, mentally handicapped people in residential care often come under a too critical scrutiny which draws undue attention to what might be perfectly normal grief behaviour, but the staff fail to recognise it as normal because their training makes them look for difficult and abnormal behaviour.

Another reason making it unwise to keep moving people around to various residential care placements and trying to assess their abilities immediately following a major bereavement is that bereavement often causes a temporary loss of abilities (see also Chapter 1) so they are likely to be functioning at a lower level of competence at this particular time and any assessment made will not do them justice. Some bereaved people who have no disabilities at all find it temporarily difficult to make a phone call or go shopping or cook a simple meal. It is as if the immensity of the loss fills the mind and leaves no room to think about or organise any other activity. For instance, Mona Clegg was a resident in a hostel for several years and visited regularly by a caring father. On the evening that she was given the news that he had suddenly died she burnt her feet quite badly whilst having a bath although she had always been very capable of bathing on her own.

Multiple losses

As people get older and their parents, friends and colleagues begin to age, their experience of loss through death increases. When a series of deaths occurs within a few months or a year the grief is hard to tolerate, and undermines confidence and brings a heightened and even frightening sense of human frailty and mortality; and each subsequent death re-activates in some degree the grief of the previous ones (see also Chapter 2).

A very sad story of multiple losses was that of sixteen-year-old Ivy. She was only fourteen when her mother died, and 15 when her father and grandmother died. When her mother had first become ill Ivy went to a short-term care hostel for occasional weeks and weekends, but when her mother died and then her father became ill she stayed at the hostel from Monday to Friday and only went home for weekends. After her father's death she became a permanent resident at the hostel.

She had three older sisters and they continued to live in the family home. The sisters and their friends were helpful to Ivy in as much as they visited her regularly in the hostel and took her back to the family home occasionally, but they were intending to sell the house so the visits there would not be for long. On one of her visits home, Ivy found that the family dog had been put to sleep, and this upset her a great deal. '*He's* gone to heaven, and mum and dad are in the cemetery' she would say whenever they passed a cemetery.

Whilst the staff at the hostel and in her school acknowledged that Ivy had suffered immense losses by both parents and a grandmother dying within two years, they found her increasingly irritable behaviour very difficult to cope with, especially when it worsened after her pet dog died. The community physician with a special interest in mental handicap expressed concern over Ivy's worsening behaviour and obvious disturbance, and wanted to organise counselling for her and some guidance for the hostel staff on how to support her. But the officer-in-charge of the hostel resisted any advice on how the hostel staff might help her, apparently seeing outside help as a form of criticism of him and his staff. So Ivy continued in her grief and disturbance, an example of how a person's grief problem may be prolonged if all the different disciplines working with people with learning difficulties do not collaborate with each other in trying to ease the bereaved person's emotional pain.

Changes of staff in a residential setting are also an experience of loss, and residents who are already grieving because of the death of a parent or other relative or a friend are likely to be disturbed by frequent changes of staff. Virginia Ryman had recently lost her father and was living in a local health service hostel. She became very attached to the charge nurse, and when he applied for another job and told the residents that he was leaving, Virginia found the impending loss intolerable and spent several days walking about the hostel crying inconsolably. The charge nurse tried unsuccessfully to comfort her. The other members of staff knew that she was upset and remarked upon it to each other over their coffee break, and even teased the charge nurse about Virginia's attachment to him. But nobody went to her and sat with her to talk about the death of her father and the impending loss of the well-liked charge nurse. It would have been more positive to have taken her aside to talk about her grief and to assign somebody on the staff to take a special interest in her; but, as so often happens in poorly organised institutions, there was a lot of chat in the staff room about the behaviour of the residents but little or no self-examination by the staff on how much responsibility they could and should take to ease the problems.

Not telling

In family life, widows sometimes do not tell their mentally handicapped sons and daughters about a death. The painful reason for this can be understood and sympathised with (see Chapter 2); it is less easy to understand and sympathise with the staff of residential care units for opting out of telling the truth. The news of a death may be hushed up and the person with a learning difficulty may not find out about it until many months later and then only in a roundabout or casual manner. Deliberate decisions not to tell are linked with the old traditional poor attitudes towards people with learning difficulties which still exist and which demean them as being too stupid or too childlike or too uncontrollable to be told the truth about important issues.

The following stories illustrate some of the various reasons that staff think they have for not giving bad news to residents.

To avoid 'trouble'

Adam Cedars was living in a health authority hostel. He was very attached to his mother and spent frequent weekends at home with her but he was not told when she became seriously ill. This was a deliberate decision taken by senior staff to 'prevent Adam causing trouble', such as breaking windows and getting into tempers. Their wish to keep the residential unit running smoothly took precedence over Adam's need for support. By withholding the news of his mother's serious illness the staff prevented him having any preparation for her possible death, and receiving support through the pain of it.

Because the person is 'too handicapped to know'
News of a parent's illness or death may be withheld from a resident because he or she has very severe multiple handicaps, being speechless, blind, and non-ambulant as well as intellectually disadvantaged. Residents in hospitals have sometimes been pointed out to me, and whispered information has been given about them, such as 'his father died last week, but he is not going to be told', or 'her mother's been dead over a year, and she still thinks every Sunday that she might come and visit. We've decided not to tell her what's happened, she won't understand.'

Staff constantly underestimate the abilities of people who cannot move or speak. But it is wrong to assume that if the person cannot ask questions they do not need to be told anything. Some staff cannot cope with the upset of breaking the news of a death to someone who cannot speak: requiring the support of responsive conversation and questions but knowing that they will not receive any verbal response to the news, they opt out of saying anything. Staff who are working in units for very severely multiply handicapped people need considerable support in giving bad news and follow-up support to bereaved residents. They need to identify with the bereaved multiply handicapped person enough to express the questions they would probably like to ask, and then try to give appropriate and comforting answers: such as where the parent died and why, who was there with them, who helped them, what is going to happen next, and so on. Ideally, in the weeks following a death, the same member of staff should reiterate the news of the loss and re-affirm the help and affection that the bereaved person can expect to get from the staff.

Because it is 'nobody's business' to tell
Sometimes a person is not told about a death simply because nobody felt that it was their business to tell them; or because staff coming on duty after time off or after a holiday do not know that the person has not been told; or because there have been changes of staff at the time of the death, and the new staff do not know that the person's relative has recently died and that they have not been told.

In large residential care settings, where many people live and work, and where there are many disciplines of staff and changes of staff, there will be rumour and counter-rumour, omissions in giving information, gossip, snippets of wrong information passed from one to another, from resident to resident, staff to staff; it is sometimes one of the mentally handicapped residents who breaks the news to another resident about a member of their family dying, having overheard the news when passing the office (for example, 'your mum has died, I heard sister talking about it on the phone in the office yesterday').

During a discussion at a meeting about grief and people with learning difficulties, a care assistant working in a social services hostel recalled that one of the residents at the hostel had suddenly become very upset many months after her mother had died, and it turned out that she had suddenly found out. The care assistant said, 'Who *told* her that her mum had died? Somebody did, but it wasn't *us*. *We* never told her. I feel guilty now when I think about it, she must have found out from one of the other residents.'

Rupert Eliot lived in a long-stay hospital. Both his elderly parents used to visit him regularly, but after his father died in 1981 his mother stopped visiting. The ward staff kept changing and although the father's death was noted in Rupert's case folder, nobody told him that his father had died and that his mother could not visit any longer because of the long journey and because she was herself too frail.

Rupert was worried for many months about what might have happened to his parents, but kept his worries to himself. Eventually he told the art therapy staff, with whom he had a good close relationship. One of the art therapists went to the ward to see if anybody knew why his parents had stopped visiting, and found out from his notes that his father had died. The ward staff had all assumed that he knew. He was then given the sad news of the death by the art therapist.

He reacted in a very normal manner; at first he shouted and denied it and swore, then he repeatedly wanted to know exactly what had happened, then wanted to know who would take his father's place and wondered whether he ought to go home and live with his mother and look after her. Later he referred to feeling guilty because once when his father had visited him he had fallen down and hurt his leg and Rupert wondered whether the fall was responsible for his father dying.

The story of Rupert is significant in that it shows that (a) in some institutions the news of a death and follow-up support may never get done by anybody, and (b) bereaved people with learning difficulties react in a very normal way to loss: they get angry, disbelieve it, want to be told repeatedly, to know all details, consider making changes in their life to help the remaining parent, and feel some guilt about the death.

To prevent bad news being discovered in painful, inappropriate ways, there needs to be clear practical instructions to staff in residential care units about who is to let the person know about a death, how it should be done, and how the follow-up support should be organised. All other members of staff who are in contact with a bereaved person with a learning difficulty — for example, domestic staff, night staff, porters and therapy staff — should also be told that he or she has suffered a loss through death. Informing all disciplines of staff who will be coming into contact with the newly bereaved person could help to prevent the sad incident that occurred in one hospital where a friendly, rather happy-go-lucky hospital porter who was collecting a multiply handicapped speechless person from a ward to take her to the occupational therapy department, teased her and said, 'Don't look so sad, you'll be off home this weekend, and your mum will spoil you, I know.' But her mother, with whom she usually spent every weekend, had been dead for three days and there would be no more weekends at home. She knew about her loss because the ward staff had told her at once and were giving her much affectionate support; but the porter had not known and could not understand the doleful expression and unusual lack of response to his jokes. She could not tell him what had happened as she was speechless. He felt very upset himself when he later found out what had happened and realised that he had accidentally caused the bereaved person unnecessary pain by his teasing.

That hospital porter and the ward staff inadvertently caused distress because there had been a lack of communication between a large number of different staff, as happened with Rupert Eliot. This is a common failing in large institutions. It is less easy to sympathise with the staff of the small hostel where Jessie Columb lived. Jessie had been living in the social services hostel for five years, and her father had been dead for more than a year but she had never been told about it because the staff colluded with each other in a massive fabrication of lies concerning the death of her father. They even continued the routine which they had when he was alive, of making a regular Saturday night evening telephone call to him from the office with Jessie sitting by their side. She was slightly deaf and had never been able to use a phone herself so she was not aware, as she sat in the office and went through the habitual Saturday night phone call, that the member of staff who was holding the phone actually had her finger on the receiver when dialling and was making up a conversation and leaving pauses when the father was supposed to be replying and sending messages to Jessie. The supposed messages were relayed to her, and she faithfully believed that he had sent them. (The ruse was known by other residents and they expressed their concern to me when I visited the hostel, saying 'it's not fair, it's not true).'

Going to funerals
The following letter from a widow expresses the uncertainty that some families feel about a person with a learning difficulty attending a funeral.

My husband died a year ago. My son Jerry, who is mentally handicapped, was 18 a few weeks before his

father died. We were all very dubious about if he
should attend the cremation. My other six children
thought 'no'. So did I at first. Then the vicar came to
see me, and he said it would be best for him to attend,
also the Head of the centre took the same view, as
Jerry was still expecting his Dad to come out of hospital. He shed a few silent tears, as his sisters were, but
I feel in my heart now I did the right thing. He comes
home one weekend a month now, from his hostel, and
for about 3 visits he asked lots of questions about Why
did Dad die? Would he see him again? Also if he could
not see him any more, would he be able to telephone?
I answered all as best as possible. Said Daddy was
happy with Jesus and his friends and in no more pain.
Since then he very rarely mentions about it, except to
say he misses him. There is always a photo here with
flowers, and he says 'that's my Dad'. I feel that if
he had never attended the funeral, he would still be
expecting him.

(Mrs Biggs)

Mrs Biggs felt that her decision was the right one.
Sometimes, however, a family requests that a son or
daughter who is resident in a hostel should not attend
the funeral of a parent or a friend, and the staff agree
without examining whether it is a good decision, and
without discussing it with the bereaved resident.
Wherever possible, however, a mentally handicapped
person should be given the choice of going; attending
a funeral can help one to accept that the death really
has occurred, as well as being an opportunity formally
to pay one's last respects.

In one large mental handicap hospital a popular
middle-aged doctor suddenly died and more than 100
residents went to his funeral service. Many of them
were deeply upset, but their attendance at his funeral
was a far more positive decision than pretending that

he had retired, moved away or gone to work in another hospital, in which case they would have felt a sense of betrayal and rejection. Knowing that he had died, recognising that the separation was out of his control and that his death was sad, was more positive than all the comfortable lies that might have been told.

People with learning difficulties living in residential care sometimes experience the death of another resident, and decisions about whether or not they should know about the death or go to the funeral are often made over their heads and do less than justice to the close friendships made between the residents and the sadness that is felt when a friend dies. When the death occurs the staff sometimes immediately clear out the dead person's possessions from the locker and room, making sure that the other residents stay away from the room until the body is taken away, and keeping the death a secret for a while. This is usually because they are themselves distressed about the death and they also wish to shield the residents from distress, thinking that if everybody gets upset it will be even harder for the staff to cope with their own feelings.

Staff with a background of general hospital training may be most inclined to do this because deaths in general hospitals are habitually hushed up; dead bodies are removed with respect but almost secretly, lockers are emptied with the bedside curtains drawn, and beds are quickly remade for other patients, and there seems to be tacit agreement between nurses and patients that they should all pretend that nothing has happened. However, in a residential care unit or a mental handicap hospital, where people live for many years as a large family, it is important that the death of a resident is spoken of openly, and that the other residents be allowed to see the body is they wish, and know where the body has been taken, and have a choice about attending the funeral and opportunities to talk about the dead person.

Twenty-three-year-old Elaine Prewett died very suddenly at a party where she had gone one evening with three friends from the home where she had been living for five years. Her friends at the home were shocked at her sudden death, but the warden in charge of the home did not allow any of the residents to go to her funeral, saying:

'they would get out of control';

'it was not necessary';

'she was not popular';

'it would be insincere as some of the residents never spoke to Elaine from one year's end to the other';

'nobody knew her'.

Quentin Archer, one of the residents who particularly wanted to go to Elaine's funeral, was described by the warden as being 'a professional mourner — morbid, and not sincere in wanting to go because he *liked* Elaine'.

The accusation of being a 'professional mourner' is a sarcastic and negative judgement that may be levelled at many people, with or without learning difficulties. Motives for going to funerals are often mixed, and can have as much to do with personal reasons and previous experiences of loss as with the actual person who has just died. Quentin had not long lost his mother and this *may* have been one of the reasons for his wanting to go to Elaine's funeral, but should not have provoked the condemnation of him being a 'professional mourner'. Perhaps the warden had his own personal reasons for not wanting to go to funerals, and used these in making decisions for the residents; or perhaps he thought of the residents as like children and did not want 'his children' to attend funerals in case they got upset or out of control.

The fear that residents might get 'out of control' or behave inappropriately is common amongst residential care staff and will be a major factor in any decisions taken about attending funerals. A fear of their own emotions may also influence the staff, perhaps making them perceive mentally handicapped people as uncontrolled, childish, uninhibited images of themselves: that is, we have learnt to control our emotions so that we do not shout or weep uncontrollably although we would like to, nor do we want to dig up our dead relatives, but we cannot be sure what a mentally handicapped person might do. (Mrs Tollman (see Chapter 4) referred to not letting her son Alan go to his father's funeral in case he wanted to dig him up). So, from mixed motives of maintaining control and the idea that people with learning difficulties should be protected from normal emotional pain, they will be excluded from funerals. Another reason for excluding them is if they are immobile, the business of having a wheelchair at the funeral being considered too much trouble, or there being difficult access to the church or crematorium; however, these factors should always be discussed with the minister and undertaker, to see how arrangements can be made.

Denial of feeling
Lack of sensitivity towards bereaved people with learning difficulties living in residential care is not necessarily a flagrant unkindness but more a *denial of feeling*. The denial or subduing of one's feelings commonly occurs amongst staff who work in emotionally stressful institutions, for example in homes for people who have physical or mental handicaps or who

are aged and dying, or in long-stay hospitals for mentally ill or handicapped persons, or the wards for sick and dying children or in hospices. Denial of feeling can result in staff ignoring the feelings of the bereaved person, and/or subduing their own rising feelings of sensitivity and tenderness. Denial may be influenced by:

1 *the size of the institution* encouraging impersonal care, with the result that nobody is responsible for setting standards of sensitivity to the individual personal needs of residents or staff;
2 *rigid staff hierarchy*: insufficient supportive contact between senior staff and junior staff;
3 *staff basic training* which emphasises physical needs and behaviour-control instead of emotional needs;
4 *lack of appropriate in-service* training for staff;
5 a belief that people with learning difficulties do not mourn;
6 members of staff finding such difficulty in coping with *their own fears of loss*, that they deny the existence or threat of loss and develop a deliberately hard-hearted attitude to other people's losses.

Denying grief may be one way of dealing with it, but it does not make for a very warm, positive and sympathetic environment. For example Eric Kingston was in charge of the North of England social services hostel where 18-year-old Dominic Hardy had recently been admitted following his mother's death. He had first been sent to an 'emergency placement' for a few nights, then he was moved into the hostel run by Eric Kingston. He must have been stunned by his loss of mother, home, belongings, life-style and two moves in rapid succession, but Eric Kingston described him as 'not reacting to his mother's death'.

Mr Kingston used the phrase 'no reaction' in reference to all the persons who were bereaved and living in his hostel. Nathan Wixley was another bereaved resident living there. His mother had dropped dead in front of him when he was home for a weekend, and he had very sensibly telephoned a relative and told them what had happened. Junior members of the hostel staff said Nathan had been 'very cut up' about his mother's sudden death, but Eric Kingston described him also as 'showing no reaction'.

It is often the senior staff who seem to manipulate a denial of feelings amongst the more junior, or inexperienced and unqualified staff, so the natural feelings of sympathy which might be extended from the latter are criticised by the seniors as being 'too much emotional involvement' and labelled as 'unprofessional'. For example, Winston, a senior member of staff in an NHS residential unit, was taking part in a discussion group when a junior member of staff asked how bereaved residents might be helped. Winston said, 'In the services, I'm an ex-marine you know, you just get used to death, take no notice. It's just a fact of life. Death does not bother me, I never worry about it.'

At another staff meeting Winston said, in reference to a resident's recent bereavement, 'Mentally handicapped people have not got the same feelings as us.' He also tended to tease the homesick residents who were in the hostel for short-term care, by saying 'your mum doesn't want you any more, she's tired of you', and at times he reduced them to tears of anxiety, whereupon he would promptly say that he was only joking. If other staff remonstrated with him about this unkindness, he would say, 'They have to get used to the hard knocks of life.'

Winston had considerable influence in encouraging

a denial of ordinary warm, sympathetic human feelings, and the younger staff who were worried about how they might cope with people with learning difficulties who might grieve for dead parents, quickly adopted his blasé attitude and took their cues from him in deciding their own manner of coping by denial.

Mr Tenby, a deputy-officer-in-charge of another NHS residential unit, was asked what he thought of several very sad stories of the adult residents who had been placed in long-stay hospitals in early infancy and had obviously suffered considerable deprivations because of their institutionalised childhoods and adolescence. He replied, 'I never read their notes, they only prejudice you about the residents.' However, by reading the old case notes he might have gained sympathetic insight into their childhood deprivations and realised that early experiences of loss might well contribute to adult reactions and insecurities. His denial of their early childhood deprivations and feelings as homesick children was a continuum of his denial of their feelings as adults.

Training in nursing and in residential care does not encourage what is dubiously called 'emotional involvement', that is, feeling deeply for the plight of a resident who may be homesick, grieving or lonely. Senior staff often discourage junior and less qualified staff from feelings of involvement or identification with the residents. The junior staff in their turn may try to damp down or divert the bereaved person's true feelings. So, somebody newly admitted to a residential care placement after a death may be expected to join in recreational activities, to jolly themselves 'out of it'. One young man, suddenly admitted to a hospital during a weekend because of a parent's death, said, 'They kept wanting me to dance, but I was too sad to.'

To have had that grieving young man happily joining in the Saturday evening dance in the hospital hall might have been one solution to the staff problems of what to do with him, but flight into jollity and activity is not the answer. He wanted to grieve, and he also wanted his grief to be recognised.

There appear to be two standards of expectations regarding emotional reactions to sad experiences, depending on whether a person has a learning difficulty or not: thus, if a person with a learning difficulty agrees to dance following a death his action will be greeted with approval and relief that he is happily occupied; but a person without a learning difficulty going to a dance immediately after a death would be disapproved of.

A form of denial which is only intended to be kind, but none the less still denies feelings, is seen in the use of inappropriate words when telling a person with a learning difficulty that somebody has died. The words 'dead', 'died', 'death' may be avoided, and 'gone to sleep', 'passed away', 'gone to Jesus', 'gone to heaven' will be substituted. Many people use these phrases when faced with the fact of a death and an irrevocable loss which at first seems too painful to admit; indeed, a walk around any English churchyard well illustrates that a large proportion of the population in the nineteenth and twentieth centuries has found comfort in muffling the fact of death in gentle description such as 'the dearly beloved husband of so-and-so, fallen asleep'; '. . . taken from us'; '. . . now living with God'. Soft phrases can be sympathised with and, in religious terms, must be respected, but always to use them to explain the death of a parent to a person with a handicap may be the cause of considerable distress. 'Going to sleep' and 'going to heaven' implies that the missing person is somewhere accessible and will eventually wake up or travel back home again. It is far kinder to use the harsher but more honest words 'dead', 'death' and 'died', for they have no other meaning than their own, and will not mislead a person into thinking that the separation is only temporary. Misleading phrases can make them feel rejected and betrayed when the dead person does not appear again.

Sometimes the truth is not told because there is a conflict between the varying interests within the residential group. This can lead to a hushing up of bad news, for fear that it will provoke questions amongst the other residents, such as 'What happens when I die?' 'Is my mum going to die, too?' 'What happens when you are buried? Do you ever get out again?' and 'Will Bill's father be burnt? will he feel it?' Painful questions like these are difficult for anybody to hear and to try and answer, and they arouse very basic fears and worries in anybody, whether they have a learning difficulty or not. A wish to protect the other members of the group, to avoid upsetting questions being asked, to avoid reminders about previous deaths, and to avoid worrying the more inarticulate members of the group, and not knowing how to cope with 'morbid questions', will result in softened but untrue phrases such as 'gone to sleep' being used.

Staff may also avoid speaking the truth because they fear that if the bereaved person has a history of violent bad tempers he or she may have some bout of uncontrollable behaviour which will cause havoc in the hostel, such as breaking windows, furniture or belongings (see also pages 87–8). And when frail physically handicapped residents are present, angry behaviour may pose a very real danger to them. However, some degree of angry behaviour is normal to bereavement and it should not be beyond the capabilities of the staff to give the angry bereaved person some organised individual attention for a while. Denial of feeling does not make the problem disappear.

The above references to denial of feeling suggest that some residential care staff are unsure about their own ability to cope with grief; they wish to appear tough to each other, and they lack appropriate leadership from their seniors; additionally, they behave in an impersonal manner towards people with learning difficulties because they do not recognise them as people with individual histories and childhood experiences. These factors encourage denial of ordinary human feelings, and will bring an undesirable and contagious atmosphere of unkindness into a residential setting.

The story of Victor Winters illustrates the misunderstandings caused when staff of residential care units do not understand the trauma of bereavement, or are afraid of what they only half-understand so take refuge in denying their feelings. Victor was aged thirty. He had Down's Syndrome, was a very capable man, and lived at home. He attended a day centre and belonged to local music clubs and had many friends in the neighbourhood. His parents had planned for the time that they would both be dead and had prepared him for leaving home by letting him visit the local hostel for people with learning difficulties whilst they were still alive and well. He had stayed there for several weekends and had good contacts there. Both his parents died within one year and Victor then moved into the hostel as a permanent home.

The staff had enjoyed his short visits whilst his parents had still been alive and had regarded him as a cheerful and popular young man. However, during his first year at the hostel following his parents' death, the staff expressed 'disappointment' about him and said that they 'could not understand why he continued to be moody and miserable for such a long time, and so different from when he used to have short visits here'. Reports on him referred to his despondency and the difficulties that the staff were having in trying to get him to 'snap out of it'. The young staff lacked any personal or professional experience of bereavement and its aftermath, and they were puzzled that Victor Winters continued to be assailed by feelings of sadness in the twelve months following his parents' death. They did not know how to cope with this new and unexpectedly morose Victor Winters and felt disappointed and resentful that he seemed so different. They would have been able to help him if they had been better informed about bereavement and recognised that his long sadness was a very normal reaction to major losses. Instead they felt themselves let down, were peeved by his misery and out of patience with what they could not understand.

Some junior and unqualified staff, without any specific training in human development or interpersonal relationships or reaction to loss, have nevertheless an empathy for grieving people and wish to console and support them; they see this as a responsibility of care staff, but they are crushed by the criticism of senior staff who tell them 'you are getting emotionally involved'.

Garry Hebden was in his forties. He had been admitted to a small residential care unit after his mother died, and he was full of sorrow and loss. An untrained member of the care staff was the most helpful person on the staff; she found time to talk to Garry, and let him talk to her about his mother, and she gradually felt that he was making a recovery. However, after a while she felt herself becoming upset and isolated, as none of the other members of staff supported her in the helpful relationship she had made with Garry; and a senior member criticised and said 'you should not have got yourself so involved', and further implied that she was 'weak, letting things get out of hand'. He meant that in her support of Garry she had given a lot of herself and shared his grief and was in need of some moral support herself. This was true; the sad thing was that none of the other members of staff were prepared to support her, although finding plenty to say in criticism.

The junior member of staff continued to feel very isolated, until a field social worker who visited the unit recognised what had been happening and used her knowledge of bereavement problems to help the young care assistant. She suggested a staff meeting, where there was an opportunity to discuss what had been happening and plan how all the staff could support grieving residents, instead of just one isolated member of the staff giving help and becoming drained by the problems. The outcome of this action was very positive and resulted in the staff drawing up a future plan of action to support the residents and each other in times of loss.

Sometimes it is not a member of the residential care staff who does the major amount of supporting a bereaved resident, but somebody of another discipline. A physiotherapist in a large mental handicap hospital was visited in her department every day for many months by a bereaved man living in one of the wards, who wanted to talk over and over again about his dead mother and be sure that he would be listened to. The physio used her lunch hour to listen to him. Nobody else was in the department at that time and she sat having her coffee and sandwiches and letting him talk. His action in seeking her out shows how in a large institution there is often a need for a quiet place and friendship so that sad things can be talked about in privacy.

Residential care staff sometimes unwittingly belittle the bereaved person's past; and people going to live in hospitals and hostels after their parents have died are often told, 'You are going to live in a nice home now' — the implication being that the previous family home was not 'nice'. Such thoughtless words can be very crushing and demeaning to the precious memories and past life. All too often the staff expect the bereaved person quickly to begin a totally new life and successfully sever all connections with the past. But bereaved people need time to let go of the past slowly. The past is a very precious part of one's identity, and needs to be respected and cherished and form a background to the future. Perhaps it is difficult for members of staff who have not had any personal experience of bereavement, to understand that bereaved people wish to talk about the dead person, they want to maintain the dead person's identity and their own by photographs and mementoes, and need to take some of the past into the future with them in order to make a recovery from their loss.

Good practices
The following examples of good practice show that if staff have empathy with the handicapped person's situation, and want to try and understand the problems of loss and its effects on a person's behaviour and happiness, they can do a lot to help even if they lack qualifications and experience.

Zena Larkin was living in a long-stay mental handicap hospital, where she had been admitted after the death of her widowed mother. She was speechless and also very physically helpless. The hospital was large, isolated, and had a reputation for poor care. Zena had never left home before and it would seem a disaster for her to be admitted to that particular hospital. However, like many of the old, traditional mental handicap hospitals, it had good and bad wards, each with its own character and style of organisation according to the staff who ran it. Zena was fortunately admitted to a loving atmosphere, albeit a crowded one with over twenty very dependent residents already living there. The staff knew that Zena had been admitted because of a bereavement and they were very sympathetic to her. One member of staff took a special interest in her so that she could be helped to feel that she still had somebody of her own. However, she did not respond to anybody on the staff, she showed little interest in her new surroundings, did not want anything to eat or drink, and began to lose weight. The staff were very concerned about her, and even wondered if she was going to pine away with grief. They were at a loss to know what to do for her as the months passed and she seemed to be visibly fading away. Then one day they took her into the ward kitchen and cuddled her on their laps whilst they had their mid-morning coffee and toast. They noticed that she perked up considerably in the atmosphere of the kitchen, with its smell of toast, and they gave her tiny bits of toast and marmite. 'It seemed that she was at home in the kitchen with the smell of cooking around her,' said the staff. 'We guessed then that her mum had probably had her in the kitchen in her wheelchair whilst she was busy, and we said, "Does this remind you of your mum, then?" and she definitely seemed to take notice.' The staff were glad to discover that going into the kitchen with them and having the extra cuddles on their laps and being able to smell the cooking and be part of a more domestic scene than in the ward day-room, was a turning point in Zena's recovery from her loss.

Maria Melville was a fairly independent person with learning difficulties living at home with her very elderly frail father. When it seemed that they needed some form of residential help Maria was found a permanent place in the local hostel for mentally handicapped people and her elderly father went with her and stayed there until he died. This compassionate decision depended on the staff's ability and willingness to nurse an elderly person and to have a death in the hostel. The hostel was in a small country community and the staff had known Maria and her father for a long time, so this probably enabled them to see them both as a family and members of the local community. After Mr Melville died, one of the staff went to see the solicitor with Maria and also to the monument shop to help her choose a headstone. The staff understood how important the grave was to her. She regarded the grave and the stone with his name on it, very normally, as a means of retaining a link with the dead person, as preserving the family identity. She knew where her father lay, near her mother, and their lives had been rounded off in a comforting way by the purchase of the memorial stone. She said, 'We won't lose the grave if it has a headstone to it and his name on it.'

Derek Lampton, aged twenty-two, was admitted to a small hostel when his mother died, and he took large quantities of family photographs with him. For many months he found comfort in going over and over the photographs with a member of staff. Less sensitive staff might have seen his quiet, rather withdrawn behaviour as morbid and depressed and might have thought it better to 'jolly him out of it', but his staff believed it was important for him to spend time looking at his photographs as an aid to his recovery from his bereavement, and they did not begrudge the time that they gave in looking at them with him. Eventually he chose one particular favourite photograph, and had it enlarged, and placed it in a very prominent place in his room. He then seemed to settle into referring to the happy memories he had of his mother and began to take part in the hostel activities. The staff felt that he had been helped to recover from his loss because he had not been hurried into activities, but had been given time to be alone if he wanted to, and had time to pore over his photographs and to think quietly about what had happened.

Edward Fenton was in his twenties and went into a small hostel after his mother died. He was obviously very grieved, but never spoke to the staff about his mother. They would have encouraged him to speak of her but he had withdrawn from them when they tried to refer to her and it was not until two years had passed that he mentioned her and referred to her dying. Even after two years he was still likely to 'clam up' if they said too much. The staff referred to how he had insisted at a recent firework party that he wanted his fireworks as he had them 'at home'. Being frustrated by a verbal disability he got cross in trying to explain, and the staff were puzzled about exactly what he wanted. However, they realised that he wanted to have his sparklers lit *outside* the window of the sitting-room and that he should watch from inside because that was how his mother had done it for him. Group fireworks out-of-doors were not in his experience, but having his sparklers outside the window as his mother had always done it made him happy. And the staff wisely did not overbearingly insist on him going outside and joining in the group and holding his own fireworks and behaving as an adult without learning difficulties; they felt that this was the first time that he had relaxed and brought some positive memory of his mother to his new situation of living in the hostel with a group, and that he should do it as he wished. He was beginning to take part yet doing it as he remembered doing it with his mother, and that was the most important thing at that stage of his recovery from his loss.

REFERENCES

1   DHSS, *Report of the Committee of Enquiry into South Ockendon Hospital* (HMSO, London, 1974).

2   DHSS, *Report of the Committee of Enquiry into Allegations of Ill-treatment and other Irregularities at the Ely Hospital*, Cmnd 3795 (HMSO, London, 1969).

3   Bowlby, J., *Material Care and Mental Health* (WHO, Geneva, 1951).

4   Robertson, J., *Young Children in Hospital* (Tavistock, London, 1958).

5   Tizard, J., King, R. D. and Raynes, N. V., *Patterns of Residential Care* (Routledge and Kegan Paul, London, 1971).

6   Oswin, M., *The Empty Hours* (Allen Lane the Penguin Press, London, 1971).

7 Oswin, M., *Children Living in Long-Stay Hospitals* (Spastics International Medical Publications, London, 1978).
8 Oswin, M., *They Keep Going Away* (King Edward Hospital Fund, London, 1984).

4 THREE STORIES

ALAN TOLLMAN

Alan Tollman was twenty-five years old and had been living for two years in Beechway, a large residential home run by the local health authority in the North of England. Twenty-five other people lived there; fifteen were permanent residents and the other ten were receiving short-term care. Alan was a very able person, he could cross a busy road on his own, was able to shop for himself and the other residents in the home, and whenever he went to visit his mother he always helped her with the housework and gardening.

Before going to Beechway Alan had lived for fourteen years in a very large mental handicap hospital. His childhood had been very deprived, he had been admitted to the hospital at the age of nine because he had been 'difficult' at school. The hospital was more than thirty miles away from his family home, but his loving parents had done all they could to keep in touch with him and had taken him home most weekends. The hospital staff had been critical of his parents' contact with him and had written 'his parents spoil him' in his case notes.

His father, who had been chronically ill for some years with a lung disease caused by industry, died a few weeks after Alan arrived in Beechway. This was a great blow to Alan as Beechway was near his parents' house and he had looked forward to moving out of the big hospital and being able to see them every day. Alan's father had always done a lot with him and they were very attached to each other. His mother felt totally unable to tell him about his father's death so asked a social worker, with whom she had a good relationship, to break the news to him. Mrs Tollman said that the people who were most helpful to her after she was widowed were the social worker and her own mother and sister. 'But nobody can really help you with your grief,' she said. 'You've got to face it on your own and get on with it alone, there's no treatment for grief.'

The following year both of Alan's grandmothers died. This was devastating for Mrs Tollman, so soon after being widowed. She told Alan about the grand-mothers' deaths herself.

Alan had not attended the funeral of his father, nor had he ever been taken to the cemetery. His mother said that her reason for not letting him go to the funeral was that she thought he 'would have been too upset, and with a burial he might have wanted to dig him up again.' The thought of this, his possible inability to comprehend what had happened and how he might behave at the funeral or in the cemetery, made her exclude him. 'I would have let him attend a cremation, but not a burial,' she said. 'With a crem-ation you see the coffin go and that is that.'

Alan's reactions, and his perception of his loss
Mrs Tollman said Alan showed a great deal of anger after his father died, swearing and shouting. Anger is a normal reaction to loss. In talking about his father

being dead his mother used the words 'gone to Jesus' and at first Alan would say, 'Can I phone him?' This wish to phone dead people seems to be particularly relevant to the way some people with learning difficulties perceive their loss; perhaps because their use of the telephone for reassurance in temporary periods of loss makes them momentarily think that they can ring somebody who has died, perceiving the death, like their other experiences of loss, as only temporary.

Alan knew that his father had died in a hospital and sometimes he would tell his mother, 'Go to hospital and get another daddy.' Perhaps this was a way of saying, 'I want a father again.' Acknowledging that his father was dead he nevertheless wanted him back; so, on one level he was accepting the death but, being verbally inept at expressing his longing for him he could only say, 'Get another daddy.' If a person with a learning difficulty is verbally incompetent other people may think that their comments about death are childish, amusing or unrealistic, but really they are attempting to 1) acknowledge the death, 2) express awareness of their loss, and 3) expressing a wish to reverse the loss ('get another daddy'). These are very normal reactions.

He also had a normal awareness of how the death had altered the shape of his family. His mother described how one day on a bus he pointed to a family and said to her, 'Look, *they've* got a Daddy,' as anyone conscious of their aloneness after a bereavement will see others in family groups, and think, 'Look, there is a mother/father/sister still in that family.'

His mother described how, on his second and third visits home after his father died, he went upstairs to the bedroom and looked in the cupboard and asked, 'Was there a ghost there?' She found this upsetting, as he had never talked about ghosts before. In asking about ghosts Alan may have been trying to understand what is meant by souls, perhaps mixing up death and souls and ghosts with something he may have seen on TV or heard at church.

When he went home he also used to search for his father. Searching is a normal reaction to loss and should not merely be associated with having a learning difficulty (see Chapter 1). This is understandable and normal grief behaviour for a temporary period of time; it would not have been normal, however, if Alan's mother had encouraged the searching or pretended that his father was coming back or could be telephoned or written to.

His mother said:

> He started to over-eat after his father died, and started filling his room with possessions . . . another thing he did was to take a great interest in plants. He'd never been interested before in plants. His dad had a greenhouse and loved plants but Alan did not show any interest. After his Dad died, however, Alan began to show a lot of interest and collected plants and had them in his room.

This again is a normal reaction, people sometimes do become very interested in the things that the dead person did (for example, gardening, photography, fishing), whereas when they were alive they took little notice.

'. . . and sometimes Alan keeps on asking me, 'Are you going to die, Mum?'

The death of a loved person brings a sense of death being around the corner, it takes away our confidence and makes us ask, will others die? Death teaches, as nothing else, a sense of mortality. So Alan, very normally, asked his mother, 'Are you going to die, Mum?'

An important stage in recovering from the impact of death is when we start to remember *happily* the things we once did together. Eventually Alan would go on the bus to town with his mother and say, 'We used to do this with Dad, he sat here,' and he would pat the seat where his father sat.

Alan's story illustrates how the perceptions of people with learning difficulties may sometimes appear distorted due to a degree of verbal ineptness, but in fact they have very normal grief reactions.

Staff attitudes to Alan's bereavements
Half the staff of Beechway had qualifications in mental handicap nursing, the other half were unqualified; all favoured a 'nursing model of care' rather than a pattern of ordinary family style residential care. Daily case-notes were kept on each resident.

As referred to above, his father died not long after Alan's arrival from the long-stay hospital to live at Beechway, so as to be nearer his parents. It was a time when the staff should have been giving particular attention to his settling in, his contact with his family and to any crises at home. His father died in the first week in June but there was no reference to the death anywhere in the case-notes that the nurses wrote at that time. The notes of 21–22 June said, 'Not in the best of moods at 07.00, threw a pillow at the bedroom wall and shouted abuse at nursing staff. Soon settled when this behaviour was ignored!'; and the notes of 23 June were: 'Alan has been incontinent of urine these past two nights.'

Alan's nursing notes throughout September and October (three to four months after his father's death) record: bedwetting, 'bad temper', 'spitting', 'hitting radiators', 'swearing', and 'attention seeking'. The suggested remedy was 'this behaviour is best ignored as it is attention-seeking'.

One may well ask what is 'attention-seeking'? A cry for help? A request for somebody to listen? A request for somebody to care? The remedy of the staff was to ignore his request, to deny his feelings and their own. The description 'attention-seeking', as it was used in Alan's nursing notes, became a condemnation; no reference was made to the need for somebody to look more closely at *why* Alan was looking for attention (help), no reference was made to him suffering a major bereavement at that time. And the steps which were recommended to cope with the attention-seeking – to ignore it and to ignore Alan (a behaviour modification technique) – would, in the instance of being bereaved, create an even greater vacuum of loss. In subsequent discussions with Beechway staff, in the course of the bereavement research, it was clear that nobody on the staff knew that bereavement could cause anger, a reduction of abilities and a craving for affection and attention.

Alan's paternal grandmother died a year after his father, and his maternal grandmother a few months later. Reference was made in his notes to the loss of his maternal grandmother, saying 'apparently not upset'. And 'difficult behaviour' was reported the next day, and in the following weeks, and he was apparently very bossy to his mother on his visits home.

In the month after the death of Alan's maternal grandmother it was noticed by other staff and residents and visitors that John (a senior member of staff) was constantly teasing him by pretending that all the staff would go away and that he would be left in charge. This worried Alan a great deal, and another resident had to keep reassuring him that it was only a joke. Such teasing would be inexcusable under any circumstances, but in view of Alan's bereavements, it amounted to mental cruelty. The threat of further losses, the disappearance of all the staff and him being left in charge, must have seemed like a nightmare.

Mrs Tollman had told me 'he was very close to his father, more so than to me really and very close to his gran who was 83 when she died'. However, at a staff meeting which was arranged to discuss my visit and the bereavement research, John said, 'Alan was not bothered about his father's death at all, not at all upset, just said to me when I came on duty, "Mr Tollman dead," and bit his hand. I reckon that he did not care at all, and was only interested in his father's death because it meant £1 a week less pocket money.' And another member of staff said, 'It was the same with his grannies' deaths, he was not upset, only upset because it meant less pocket money.' These condemnations by Beechway staff were prejudiced and unjust, and illustrated their lack of understanding of bereavement.

It was curious that, when there was some suspicion of Alan 'indulging in homosexual and heterosexual activities', an urgent staff meeting was called, a long discussion ensued, a plan of action was drawn up and all the staff were informed of it. Yet the death of his father never merited a mention anywhere in his notes, and the death of his maternal grandmother received merely a laconic 'apparently not upset'.

Eleven out of the fifteen permanent residents at Beechway had had experiences of bereavement in the previous two years, but the staff showed a singular lack of interest in bereavement problems, none of them had had any training in the understanding of bereavement, and even those with personal experiences of loss seemed unable to bring that insight to the situation for the bereaved residents of Beechway. It would appear that it was easier to deny their feelings and follow the general leadership of ignoring the effects of loss.

PEGGY BENCHLY

I met Peggy Benchly when she was 68. She had just been admitted to a small hospital for people with learning difficulties in South-East England. She was at that time very frail and in poor health, and needed nursing care. She was not expected to recover from the several illnesses of premature old age from which she was suffering. Her widowed sister, Mrs Joyce Cossett, was spending the greater part of the day in the hospital sitting by her bedside, and over a number of days she told me Peggy's story.

Peggy had always had a very loving family life. Her father had died in the 1930s when she was 19 years old. She had continued living at home with her mother. She was 35 years old when her mother died, and she then went to live with her sister and brother-in-law, Mr and Mrs Cossett, and their three-year-old little girl. She lived with her sister for 34 years, until her admittance to the mental handicap unit for terminal nursing care.

Mrs Cossett said she had always been determined that her sister should never be sent away to live in an institution. She recalled how once, many years ago in the 1940s, a local group of mentally handicapped children and their families all went on a coach outing as a nice day out, and, on the way, one of the small children in the coach was actually admitted to a big institution for over 1,000 retarded people. It had apparently been convenient to use the coach trip to deliver the child to the institution as it was out in the countryside and difficult to get to by public transport. But the incident had dampened the spirits of all the others. Mrs Cossett and the rest of the family were adamant that nothing like that should ever happen to Peggy and, in the 34 years since their mother had died, they had succeeded in having her living always at home within the family.

Peggy was with her mother when she had died very suddenly after collapsing in the bedroom. She was told that her mother was dead and the words 'passed away' were used. She went to live with her sister and her husband immediately after her mother died. Her sister said that as Peggy had never slept on her own and was used to sharing her mother's bedroom, she and her husband let her sleep in their room rather than distress her.

If Mrs Cossett ever got ill with flu or a heavy cold, Peggy would get very worried and say to her, 'Your face won't go white, will it?' She could vividly recall witnessing her mother's sudden death, and for two years afterwards she had bad bouts of crying, especially when she was having her periods which was always a time for her feeling low.

Peggy's two years of occasional weeping and her worries about other people getting ill and dying, and her vivid remembering of her mother's appearance in death, were very normal reactions to bereavement. Her worry about the likelihood of her sister also dying is another common anxiety after a bereavement; death takes away confidence, and makes people aware of their own and other people's mortality. It is very normal to worry about the people who are important to us and ask ourselves, 'Will you die, too, and you and you?'

In the months after their mother's death, if Peggy began crying and saying, 'I miss Mum,' Mrs Cossett and the other members of the family comforted her by saying, 'You've got *Betty*, you've got *Alice*, you've got *Joyce*,' saying the names of the three sisters to her and holding up their fingers and pointing to themselves as they did so. Mrs Cossett said that they had all tried to keep the family memories vivid to her, and they would look at family photos together and talk about things that had happened 'at No. 38' (the parents' house) and use the family catchphrases and jokes.

Peggy was helped to recover from her mother's death and the changes it made in her life, because she went to live with her sister and her husband and had other members of the family around her. In having the family memories kept alive for her she also retained her own identity and this gave her additional security. Had she gone into a large institution after her mother died she would inevitably have lost her identity, and it would have been hard for her to recover from her bereavement.

Being a member of a family also helped her to perceive her new situation; for example, when Mrs Cossett's little girl sent her mother a Mother's Day card Peggy said to her sadly and quite crossly, 'You lucky, *you*, you've got *two*, a Mum and a Dad, I've got *none*, you lucky you are.' Within a normal family setting and mixing with people of varying ages, she was able to think about age and loss, and the advantages that young children seem to have, in a way which would not have been possible had she been living in a segregated institution where there would have been no pattern of family life.

As the years passed there were inevitably other bereavements – sister Betty died when Peggy was aged 53; she had been ill for a very long time and all the family knew that she was not going to recover. Peggy was told about Betty's death, and 'cried a great deal'. However, a year later, when Alice died very unexpectedly of a stroke in her sleep, she was not told. 'I never told Peggy about Alice dying, it would have been too much for her to cope with, it was so sudden,' said Mrs Cossett. Whenever Peggy asked, 'Where's Alice?' the rest of the family would say 'gone to see Freda' (a niece). It was the shock and suddenness of Alice's death which made it difficult for her family to break the news to Peggy, whereas it had been easier when Betty died because she had been ill for a very long time. When Peggy was 57 Mrs Cossett's husband died. Again, Peggy was never told. Mrs Cossett found that it was too upsetting to speak to Peggy about her husband's death so she actually told her that he had gone to France, and for some years Peggy wrote little letters to him and Mrs Cossett pretended to post them.

It may seem out of character for Mrs Cossett, who had shown what might be called 'good common sense' about their mother's death and the first of her sisters' deaths, to have been so secretive and dishonest about the death of her second sister and her own husband. However, there can be no exact expectation of certain behaviour when a death occurs. As circumstances in a family alter, so may each new experience of death be reacted to differently. Mrs Cossett had been younger at the time of their mother's death and there had been the two other sisters still alive and her own husband to support her. But as she became elderly and lost more and more members of her family, it became increasingly hard for her to cope with her own griefs and to be confident in comforting Peggy. And the most difficult of all the deaths was that of her husband, who had been most loving and stalwart in helping her to cope with all her previous losses.

So, becoming elderly and experiencing severe loneliness as more and more members of her family died, Mrs Cossett eventually started to make up stories about her dead sister and husband, and found comfort herself in pretending to Peggy that they were both alive. Once a story starts, it will be encouraged by social isolation and by the presence of a person with learning difficulties who believes the story.

MAVIS OSBORNE

Mavis Osborne was born in 1943 and went to an ESN school, a local education authority school for children who were categorised at that time as being 'educationally subnormal', under the 1944 Education Act. She had a variety of unskilled jobs after leaving school: in restaurants, laundries and kitchens. But she was always being sacked from these jobs because of getting into tempers. Eventually she went to a day centre for mentally handicapped people and then into a long-stay hospital. After three years in the hospital she went back home to live with her parents and then moved with them to the country when they retired.

In the 1970s, Mavis Osborne was in her thirties and living with her parents and attending what was then known as an Adult Training Centre for Mentally Handicapped People, but she had some distress and trouble there after the family dog died. She became depressed and began to get into tempers. Her only interest in this depressed state was going for long walks with a relative (perhaps reminiscent of the happy walks with her dog). She had liked television but stopped watching it in her sadness about her dead pet. Three months later a community physician specialising in mental handicap visited her at home. Mavis produced a photograph of her dog to show him. She was obviously depressed at the loss of the loved pet. The death of a pet can make an impact which should not be underestimated; it is often the first experience of loss that anybody has, and, if handled badly, denied, or ignored, may have depressing effects, and colour one's subsequent experiences of loss.

The community physician could not offer any solution to her upset, and six months after losing her pet she was admitted to a big long-stay hospital. After living for eight years in that hospital she was given a place in a NHS residential home called Rippledale which had just opened in the town where her parents lived and had accommodation for thirty people.

She arrived at Rippledale with a reputation for being 'awkward'. The attitudes of the hospital staff towards her had apparently been strongly influenced by the behaviour modification techniques which were so much the fashion in the 1970s. Staff had reacted very punitively to any sign of bad behaviour, for example they had once taken away her scented soap as a punishment, but when she erupted into tempers over this treatment they had sedated her.

Her notes from the hospital referred to an acquired habit of keeping one eye shut. Her mother had written to the hospital about this, because she was worried about the effect on her appearance and sight. The doctor had decided that the way to break this habit was to tell Mavis that her mother was too worried to have her home again unless she kept both eyes open. He wrote in her notes, 'Her home visits are a great reward to her and we can reinforce this in the hospital.' This example of behaviour modification, categorising her visits home as a 'reward' and threatening to withdraw them unless 'good behaviour' was ensured, and using the visits as 'reinforcement' of what was considered to be acceptable social behaviour, gives a tragic example of professionals threatening a woman with severe loss if she did not break a habit which really did no harm to anyone. The misuse of behavioural techniques (threats of punishment, threats of group disapproval, pressure to conform otherwise one would be deprived of something pleasurable, threats of loss) was common at that time and bordered on mental cruelty.

Not long after Mavis arrived at Rippledale her uncle died of cancer after a long illness. She had been very fond of this uncle and upset at seeing him deteriorate and was very distressed when he died. It was about this time that she began to be described by Rippledale staff as 'morbid and too interested in illness and death'. She was perturbed about another resident's terminal illness and tried to speak to the staff about it. She also wanted to talk about two other residents she knew who had died 'after getting ill like my uncle'. The staff said they were trying to ignore her questions and thought that they should discourage her from 'being morbid' and talking about illness and death. Her awareness of death and sensitivity to the fact that long illnesses and physical weakness sometimes resulted in death were firmly stamped on by the staff.

During my visits to Rippledale several meetings were held with residents and staff to talk about personal experiences of loss, and different forms of loss.

Mavis Osborne could have made a positive contribution to the discussion, and might also have obtained some comfort herself by sharing her knowledge of loss, but the charge-nurse decided to exclude her from the meeting, 'as she was inclined to be too morbid anyway.' A junior member of staff later said she thought that some knowledge of the meeting had 'filtered through' to Mavis because the next time she went home she brought back with her a photograph of her dead uncle. Perhaps, having heard about the bereavement meetings taking place, she hoped that she could come to talk about her uncle and show us all his photograph.

It was sad to see from Mavis's story that her losses were never acknowledged, and her attempts to make contact with other people and talk about her feelings were constantly rebuffed and seen only in terms of 'awkward behaviour' or 'being morbid'. In that residential unit she was a key person with experience of loss, but nobody on the staff had taken the opportunity to help her, or to make positive use of her experiences to help others or to enrich their own knowledge. She had met only with rebuff and criticism, and exclusion from the bereavement meetings which she could have contributed to and would have found helpful.

5 TALKING ABOUT LOSS

> I used to look after my mum, she needed drinks
> making for her. She couldn't get out of bed. I did
> the housework, and cooked things. People came
> in and helped every day. She was poorly for two
> years. When she died I went to live in the hostel.
> But there is nobody there for me to look after. I
> miss doing things for my mum. I liked looking
> after her. I did not get worn out by looking after
> my mum. I liked doing it.*

This woman, aged in her forties, was trying to adapt
to the changes in her life since her mother died. She
was coping very bravely, but her personal grief, and
her need to talk about her loss and to have help in
filling the gap left by her mother's death were not
sufficiently recognised by the professionals who were
in contact with her. It is possible that the caring role
of people with learning difficulties is underestimated.
Her independence and sense of usefulness were being
eroded by her institutional life.

During the research several meetings were held
with the staff and residents of residential units, to
discuss the problems caused by bereavement, loss and

* Oswin, M., 'Nobody for me to look after', in *Parents
Voice*, March 1982.

change. The residents who attended the meetings had a variety of abilities and background experiences, some being severely handicapped by multiple disabilities and communication disorders, and others being very able and independent. Many had lived for twenty to forty years in long-stay institutions but some had only just come into residential care from their family homes. The majority had had bereavement experiences, either through parents and relatives dying, or friends and staff in the institutions.

In deference to those residents who appeared to have severe difficulties in understanding, I would begin the meetings by simply saying that the meeting was about how we felt when we were sad and who could help us when we were sad. I suggested that we might be sad because we had lost something or had had a disappointment; or because somebody had died, which was the worst sadness of all.

The following account is of a meeting held in a 16-bedded hostel, attended by eleven residents and a social worker. All of us had had at least one experience of bereavement.

Joe Murphy started off with a very articulate speech in which he said, 'Everybody has to die at some time, we are very very sad when it happens but we have to make a life of our own then and do the best we can. We should try to describe how we feel from our heart.'

Rachel Thomas, whose sister had died two years before, said that she was very worried about her mum and dad, who were now in their eighties and nineties. She was very sympathetic towards her parents for having lost a daughter, and said how awful it was that she had died. She also said how she would like to be living with them, to try and help them, instead of living in the hostel.

She then spoke about how worried she felt about her own future when she no longer had a mother. She was not only worried about her mother being poorly and her father aged 94, but was worried about herself when she would be finally alone and without any family at all. Her sister's death had aroused her awareness of her parents' mortality and made her feel worried about her own vulnerability and likely future loneliness.

Rachel seemed depressed about her future. She was in her 40s, had multiple physical handicaps as well as learning difficulties, and had lived in institutions since adolescence. She had a voluntary visitor, but said that she did not think she would be able to keep this nice person as a permanent friend:

'You see, I'm shy and I have not got much to say and I think they will not think I'm very interesting so won't come any more to see me.'

Rachel had a sad lack of confidence in her ability to keep a friend; she could not believe that she had anything much to offer anybody to make them want to continue visiting her. Her worries about losing her visitor seemed also linked to her worries about losing her parents. Perhaps she felt that when they were gone there might be nobody else to love her and understand her in the same way. She could not believe that a voluntary friend would ever see her as a person to care about and continue visiting.

She was looking ahead to the time when she would be alone and was clearly asking herself if she could ever make somebody love her as her parents loved her. She said she had not been able to talk about this before because she 'had not had a chance to do so'. The fears which she expressed about the future were both touching and disquieting, and raised the question of why nobody had helped her to talk about this before. It would seem that some people with multiple disabilities and learning difficulties should be given definite opportunities to discuss these very personal matters.

Eve Johnson spoke about her father who had been very ill with cancer. She said, 'I had a telephone call to say he had passed away. He died of cancer ... but my mum still has my sister and my aunties, so she's not on her own. I was not allowed to go to the funeral in case I got upset. I don't like funerals.'

The social worker at the meeting then asked her if she had ever been to a funeral. Eve said not, and repeated that she did not like them. Her words suggest that professionals may be passing on their own fears and prejudices to people with learning difficulties. In this way the bereaved person will be encouraged to make a choice which conveniently fits in with what is being organised for them, that is, the staff and Eve's family preferred that she should stay away from the funeral, so they suggested to her that she did not like funerals.

Joe Murphy then said that he had found his first Christmas without his mother very lonely. She had died in the November.

'She was not there, I did miss her sitting there with us. But the next Christmas had not been so difficult, the first one was the worse one of all for me.'

He was very keen to share with other people his feelings and memories about his mother. He had brought her photograph to the meeting, also a diary, and a newspaper cutting announcing her death.

He said that when his mother was dying two members of the hostel staff had made it possible for him to visit the hospital three times a day. They had to get special permission for him to do this from the sister of his mother's ward. Joe obviously appreciated the help he had been given by the staff and referred to how they had at first tried to dissuade him from visiting in case he got upset, but when he had insisted they had helped him all they could.

Richard and George Knowles, both aged in their 40s, talked about Alf, the man who had lived with their mum for more than thirty years. He had died two years ago and they had been told by a member of the nursing staff. George wanted to talk about Alf's death in a matter-of-fact way, but Richard said he did not like to talk about it nor to think about it.

'It is so sad, I still feel sad about Alf, and don't want to talk about him now. If I talk about him I might cry and I don't want that,' he said.

'But I cried every day about my mum,' Joe Murphy said.

'Sometimes it is difficult for men,' I said, 'they feel they should not cry in front of other people. Is that how you feel, Richard?'

'Yes,' Richard replied: 'I cry about Alf on my own, tears come down out of each of my eyes.'

At a later meeting in that hostel a nineteen-year-old severely handicapped young woman called Beth, who had been at a previous meeting and had not appeared to understand anything, opened the discussion by suddenly saying, 'last time we talked about how we cope when we lose somebody.' As I agreed with her and remarked on her good memory, twenty-year-old Bob, another very handicapped person, called out, 'Jim dead.' (Jim was a former resident who had died there recently.)

Both these severely handicapped young adults were

very quiet and not very competent verbally, but had obviously been interested in the previous meetings, and had understood perfectly well that the discussion was about loss and death and coping with grief, and were able to relate the discussion to their deceased friend Jim. Their interested response at the follow-up meeting suggests how easy it is to underestimate people who have severe learning difficulties.

The staff who were present expressed surprise that Bob and Beth had understood what we had been talking about. They had wanted to select for the meeting only those residents whom they thought would understand what our discussions were about and those who could contribute with some verbal competence, and had suggested leaving out Beth and Bob.

At our meetings we talked about varieties of loss, not only loss through death. The social worker brought up the subject of staff leaving, and we listed ten people who had left from the staff of the hostel, or from the centre or the church which the residents attended.

We talked a lot about people always moving on and staff leaving to go and work in different places. Several people referred to Eve Johnson having been very upset at a recent fête because she knew that Clive, the charge nurse, was leaving. I was prepared to skate over staff moves, not wanting to make it appear that they cared so little about the residents that they did not want to stay. But George Knowles suddenly said, baldly and with surprising cynicism, 'People change jobs so as to get more money.'

Most of the residents seemed to think that their relationships with staff were often very shallow and based on nothing more than a need to earn money. This may have been because staff had honestly explained to them that people only leave because they want better jobs and more money. This had inevitably made them feel that caring relationships could be broken off very quickly when there was a promise of more cash somewhere else.

We talked about another form of loss being when residents move from one hospital or home to another. They referred sadly to friends who had been left behind in hospitals, and long friendships broken off by moves from the big long-stay hospitals where they had lived together for twenty or thirty years or more.

Eve Johnson spoke about Christine, her friend whom she had left behind in a long-stay hospital. She said, 'I don't know what has happened to her.'

Joe Murphy spoke about his blind friend Doreen. She too had been left behind in a long-stay hospital. Joe said that he used to ring Doreen up for a while after he had moved out of the hospital. But the staff had said that his phone calls were 'upsetting her' and the sister of Doreen's ward eventually told him not to ring any more.

It was of some concern to note that people with learning difficulties were being moved around to different residential units, and were not always helped or encouraged to keep in touch with old friends. It would seem important that the staff of the old hospitals and those working in new residential units should help the residents to keep in touch with old friends by phone calls, letters and visits.

* * *

At a meeting held in a long-stay hospital, Hilda Smith, a resident who had an evening job in a local pub, referred to the owner of the pub being recently widowed. Hilda had been close friends with the couple for some years. She said she cried when she saw her friend's husband lying dead. Since the death she had continued to go to see her widowed friend and she still helped her in the pub. She said, 'I like to keep her company, and talk to her, it helps her to have company.' There was general agreement that 'keeping a person company', and talking to them was helpful. The following comments were made by the group:

'We are sad when people die';

'we are lonely';

'friends can help';

'when people are kind and talk to us, are friends, it helps the loneliness and sadness'.

They also talked about the number of very elderly residents who had recently died. One very popular long-stay resident had just died at the age of 90. 'I've been to so many funerals this year,' said Vicki Walsh, a resident who was in her late 70s.

In any long-stay institution it is inevitable that there will be groups of elderly residents who have been institutionalized since childhood or adolescence and have grown up together, leading enclosed lives; perhaps sharing, for 40 years or more, dormitory-type sleeping accommodation and communal dining-rooms and sitting-rooms. Growing old together, reaching their eighties and nineties, these long-stay residents will, as Vicki Walsh said, begin to experience several deaths a year. Large groups of similar-age people growing old together are a peculiar characteristic of the old-style institutional living. The effect of seeing their long-known friends gradually die must be very depressing. Very little is known about what might here be called 'institutional bereavement' (it occurs commonly in homes for elderly persons, geriatric wards, and hospices), but it is only in the old large mental handicap hospitals and psychiatric hospitals that the members of the group who are experiencing this 'institutional bereavement' would have lived together for as long as twenty, thirty or forty years or more.

JOE MURPHY'S OWN STORY

Joe had spent many years in a long-stay mental handicap hospital. I met him shortly after two of his friends, Jim and William, had died. They had lived in the long-stay hospital with him, and the three of them had been discharged together to live in the sixteen-bedded hostel in the city from which they had originated and where their families were still living. Joe said:

'Just talking to Jim the night before, we said, "well, we're off to bed now." I said goodnight to him, he said goodnight to me, see you tomorrow and then he died.'

He referred with some astonishment to the fact that dying can suddenly be part of everyday life, that one can be 'only just talking to somebody' the day before and the following day the person may be dead. He showed the same disbelief as most people do, of how suddenly a person can be dead, somebody with whom one shared a room, went to work with or saw in the evenings.

Joe said he always slept with his door open and, on the night of Jim's death had become aware of 'something up – the nurses were hurrying about and there were ambulance men and a lot of noise . . . and in the morning the staff came to the *sensible* ones and told them.'

The staff selected certain residents to tell. Some were not told. (How did they make this choice and on what criteria? Was it based on the nuisance value of likely reactions? Or on assumptions of ability to understand?)

Joe had known William and Jim very well as they had lived together in a big institution for many years, and also their parents were friends. 'We were not pushed to go to the funeral, but I went. I wanted to go. The staff did not push us.' He seemed philosophical about his friends' deaths and when I suggested that perhaps it was sad to speak about them he said, 'We've got to go one day, we can't live forever.'

Joe's mother had died two years before I met him. He wanted to talk about her, although it made him upset. When he referred to her he used none of the common philosophical explanations (such as 'we've all got to go') that he used in reference to William and Jim.

His mother 'had lots of strokes' and died shortly after Joe had been discharged from the big hospital and moved into the small hostel.

He said:

'I promised my mum I'd go to her bedside if she was ill. I kept my promise. But when I saw her she couldn't speak. She heard me, I know she heard me. I loved my mum, I really did. I kept my promise to her.

'Then on Saturday I was outside waiting for my brother to come to take me home and there was a phone call and it was to say she'd died. Nurse Irene told me and I collapsed and cried and cried. I couldn't stand, I collapsed and they had to get a wheelchair. And they put me in the wheelchair and took me to my bedroom and gave me a cup of tea and put me to bed, and I could not stop crying. I loved my mum, I really did, I cried for days.

'I went to the funeral, it was my wish to go. There were lots of flowers, I only had to see the flowers there

and I collapsed again. I was talking to the vicar afterwards and I saw the flowers and started to cry and
collapsed again, and they sat me in the car.'

He said that the social worker who was attached to
the hostel went with him to see his family because he
wanted to pay his share of the funeral expenses. 'Phil
[the social worker] spoke for me, said I wanted to pay
my share, I was entitled to pay my share, to do my
duty to put something towards the funeral. We each
gave £20.'

It appeared that he or Phil had anticipated that the
rest of the family might not let him contribute to the
funeral. But he wanted to and was glad that she had
helped him to express this view. Each year now he
puts an 'In Memory' notice in the local paper, being
advised on how to do so by the same social worker who
had supported him through his bereavement.

Joe had fairly severe learning difficulties but his
story described very normal reactions to bereavement.
For instance the loss of long-known acquaintances,
although sad, may be helped by the philosophical
clichés everyone tends to use at times to explain death
(like 'we've all to go'). But the loss of people whom we
love very much (parents or very close friends) causes
severe grief; comfort may then be derived from the
fact that one kept one's promises to the loved one
such as having been at their bedside; and it becomes
important to attend the funeral and contribute to the
cost. Joe's story differed from the norm in that it was
necessary for him to ask a social worker to be his
spokesman in putting his views to his family.

THE STORY OF RODNEY WEEKS

Rodney Weeks's mother died four years before I met him. She had died in his arms suddenly in their kitchen. After spending the first week at a neighbour's house he was sent to a social services hostel as an emergency. He stayed there for 18 months.

Morag, the deputy head at the social services hostel, was very concerned about Rodney's bereavement. She said that during his first year in the hostel he would frequently burst out crying and say how much he missed his mother. Morag wanted to help Rodney. As his birthday approached he became very upset, and said, 'Who will make my birthday cake for me – I won't have one any more.' Morag promised that he *would* have one because she would make it for him. At the same time she said that she 'could not replace your mum, but I can be your friend'. She made the cake for him, with him helping.

The way in which Morag helped Rodney through his loss was very sensitive. He was allowed to show his grief, and was given individual attention and support, especially in the making of his birthday cake. Whenever possible, the maintenance of old family ceremonies is very important. People often yearn for the old routines when the person who organised them has died. (See also Edward – pages 108–9.)

Another member of the hostel staff said that Rodney had 'shown more worry than most mentally handicapped people about his mother dying, he has also been worried and anxious about his uncle dying.'

After a major bereavement it is normal to worry over the possibility of more people dying. One is frightened that the experience will recur, death seems to undermine one's confidence so that nothing feels safe any more. (See also Queenie, p. 56.)

After Rodney's mother died he tried to make contact with relatives who had not been much in contact, for example cousins and uncles. Whatever the outcome of this searching for out-of-touch relatives, it is a very common and normal reaction, a form of trying to reconstruct family life and thus restore one's identity.

The following story of Rodney is in his own words, as dictated to Morag.

> The following is an account of Rodney's life *in his own words* as he told it to me . . .
>
> My name is Rodney Weeks. I was born in Dale Road, Plymouth. I had a rocking horse when I was a baby. I used to like it. I went to the Ernesettle Primary School but I was slow at learning and then I was transferred to Mount Tamar (a special school) when I was six. From there I went to Highbury (a day centre). I can't think what my teacher was called. I ran away from school one day, me, Valerie and Bernice. Valerie threw a shoe out the window so the teacher couldn't chase us. The 'cops' was looking for us and one of the coppers said 'where are they little buggers to?' There was cops everywhere, we was hiding in the park. The police found us 2 o'clock in the morning. I had a hiding from my Dad, it was sore, flipping heck it was. The next day the teacher told us off and also I put books down the back of my trousers so it wouldn't hurt. I hated PE because we used to get in with the girls, I liked to play basket ball.
>
> I was about eleven when I went to Highbury – I liked it at Highbury. I liked reading and writing. I can't read much. Some words I can. I used to stay home from school a lot 'cause my mum was ill with a bad back. I had to help her get around every time she moved it hurt her.

My dad taught me things at home. He used to take me out. I had a sister called Sonia, she was killed before I was born, see my mother was going across the courtyard and a bomb came, one that was called a buzz-bomb and it blew the roof off, she was trapped, they tried to save her but it was no good, she was suffocated. When it happened my Dad was in the Navy in Malta and 'course he had a special telegram see to come home. When he had the telegram it really shook him up see really up. Sonia is buried up by the Rectory at Overton Gifford. My Mum and Dad cried a lot, they are bound to aren't they?

When I was born in 1946 the War was over and finished with, but Dad was still in the Navy, he stayed for two years more see because there was no jobs course Plymouth was badly bombed.

He was a barracks gardener Dad was for three or four years, he came off that because he had bronchitis and went to Wembury to work. He was a civilian driver driving the Navy boys around, he liked it so much, all his mates was at his funeral. My Dad died in 1972, I felt awful, rotten I did. I still do now. I loved him a lot, I still do you see. He used to take me everywhere, he had a motorbike and used to meet me from school and take me home. We used to go to football.

My dad was the greatest and my Mum was. Vi across the road broke her heart when Mum went. The night mum died, I panicked like anything I really did, of course I think myself she choked on her tongue. I just opened the flippin back door to let her go out to the toilet and she flipping fell back in my arms. I said 'Oh God no don't let her be gone.' I ran for Vi and George over the road, they came across, they tried to get the doctor but couldn't so got another one, then the pathologist come. I was crying 'I want my Mum.' Vi took me over her house, my Uncle Norman came to Vi's, then the undertaker come, they put her in a black thing, I was in the other room and saw them. This black thing was zipped up, because there's a lot of nosey parkers in that area see. I stayed at Vi's house for a couple of weeks until they found me a place. I used to go out to the club from Vi's and go out to work from her house. I came to Welby, I really love all the staff here, Mr Price, Mrs Lyddon, Mrs Nicholas and Mrs Davis. I do I really do, if it wasn't for you I don't know where I'd be.

I think that when someone dies I think to myself they are up there watching me, there some is up there. I feel Mum, Dad and Sonia are all together, that's what I think, I hope so anyway.

I go to the St George's Training Centre, I tried to get other jobs. I went down the Bush and they didn't want to know because of where I worked, because they knew I was very slow. I could have done that flippin job, it was sweeping up, you know, cleaning up the floors. My Dad tried to get out of the training years ago, there was a job at Wembury Camp, washing the vehicles, I didn't get it because of the same reasons.

At St George's I work for three days a week on the car wash. I like it, I talk to the men and they are friendly. The other two days I work in the kitchen, I work the machine that peels the spuds, they come down a shoot and go into the sink, they somebody else takes all the black bits off them. I like my job.

I like to go out and meet my friends and have a shandy. I help at the Agaton Social Club on a Saturday night, I get a taxi back from there and the club pays for that.

I'm leaving Welby soon to go to a new place, Durnford Street, Stonehouse. I will miss the staff here, I'll miss them a lot. I am looking forward to my new life, hope it's OK.

I dream that one day I'll get another job and be prosperous.

(Morag Lyddon and Rodney Weeks)

**How a bereaved person who could not speak
was helped**

It is very difficult to know how to help a bereaved
person who is speechless. Sometimes there is little
more that one can do except hold them, make sure
that they see familiar people if possible, try to find out
about their past routines and keep to them in the
new situation, and always talk to them honestly. The
following account is of how one professional helped a
grieving person who was profoundly handicapped and
speechless.

Lilian Travers, a social worker attached to a residential unit for people with learning difficulties,
described a 45-year-old woman who was suddenly
admitted because her mother had died. She was profoundly handicapped and speechless and had never
left home before. Lilian explained the death to her by
showing her a photograph of her father who had died
16 years earlier and explaining that her mother had
now died too. A few days later the social worker
requested that her mother's clothes should be sent to
the hospital so that she could go through them with
the bereaved daughter. She cried bitterly when she
saw the mother's clothes. 'She stroked her mother's
brooch and cried for a long time,' said Lilian. Although
the breaking of the news was so painful to the
bereaved woman and to the social worker, the sensitive manner in which it was done was very supportive.
She had been given an honest explanation of what
had happened. She had looked at photographs of her
parents and had her mother's death linked to her earlier experience of bereavement when her father had
died. She had been shown her mother's clothes, and
been allowed to grieve over them, with somebody present to comfort her.

The discussions which were held showed the normality of the residents' individual reactions when experiencing losses.

For example:

a) Rachel Thomas referred to her own vulnerability – an experience of death bringing thoughts of other people's deaths and one's own mortality, and emphasising one's aloneness.

b) The sadness felt about anniversaries – Joe Murphy's first Christmas without his mum was the worst.

c) Joe Murphy could speak openly about his loss, whereas Richard Knowles was afraid to speak about such things in case he cried; he was afraid of his own sadness and felt the need to be 'brave' and not expose his sadness.

d) Eve Johnson and Rachel Thomas were sensitive to their parents' losses and were able to see what it meant to them to lose a husband and a daughter.

e) They were all aware of what it meant to lose close friends when moving from one residential unit to another.

The differences between experiences of loss for people *without* learning difficulties and those *with* learning difficulties was shown not in the reaction of the latter group but in their vulnerability and in other people's attitudes towards them. For example:

i) Rachel Thomas felt that she was very much alone although living in a group;

ii) Moves from one institution to another meant they had little or no control over keeping contact with former friends;

iii)   They were sometimes given no choice of attending funerals;

iv)   They were sometimes not told of deaths;

v)   Because of staff change they experienced constant losses of people they had become fond of, and had little means of retaining contact.

6 RECOMMENDATIONS AND SUGGESTIONS

There is only one kind of shock worse than the totally unexpected: the expected for which one has refused to prepare.

Mary Renault, *The Charioteer*, 1953

When a person with learning difficulties dies their surviving parents sometimes say: 'He is safe now, we wanted him to die before us, now we won't have to worry any more about ourselves dying and leaving him — we know he is safe now.'

These sad words express the lack of confidence that most parents feel about the services provided by their local health authorities and social service departments. It is a terrible indictment of public services, if families feel that their sons or daughters are better dead that living without parents and being the unhappy recipients of inappropriate services.

The following recommendations and suggestions give ways in which people with learning difficulties might be supported when they are bereaved. In the recommendations it is usually parents who are referred to as being the deceased, but it could equally be a sibling, cousin, grandparent, close friend, or husband or wife whom the person with a learning difficulty is mourning.

Learning

1 In-service training courses on bereavement should be available for professionals working with people who have learning difficulties.

2 Other connected professionals and persons should be able to attend the courses: district nurses, family doctors, undertakers, church ministers, advocates, volunteers.

3 Professionals working with people with learning difficulties should endeavour to link up with local groups of CRUSE and Compassionate Friends, to share information.

4 Staff working in day centres or residential settings should use spontaneous opportunities for teaching about death, for example, when politicians, screen stars or sportsmen die, or a death occurs in a popular TV series.

5 A person with a learning difficulty should have their questions about death answered with respect and honesty.

Breaking the news of a death

6 The news of a death should be given with honesty and not hurriedly.

7 Some persons may be comforted by being cuddled when bad news is given to them.

8 The correct language of death should be used – dead, dying, died – as these words have only one meaning, unlike 'gone to sleep' or 'passed on' which may be misleading.

9 News of a death should not be withheld because

it is thought that a person is either too handicapped to understand or may react with violence.

10   Professionals and relatives should never pretend
that a dead person is still alive.

Going to funerals

11   People with learning difficulties should be given
the same opportunities as other members of their
family to go to the funeral and to be at the graveside or the crematorium.

12   A person should not be excluded from a funeral
because it is thought that they will not understand or will get upset.

13   Family worries about the feasibility of a person
with learning difficulties attending a funeral may
be resolved by the person having the assistance
of a professional, an advocate or a volunteer
accompanying them.

14   If the person has severe multiple disabilities and
is immobile a relative or professional should make
sure beforehand that the funeral car can take a
wheelchair and that there is good access to the
church, the graveside or crematorium.

15   A person with a learning difficulty should be
given an opportunity to buy their own flowers for
the funeral or to contribute in other ways
requested, and appropriate help should be given
in doing this.

16   If a group of people from a centre or hospital are
attending a funeral they should not go in a minibus like an outing: cars are expensive but are
more respectful and normal.

Acknowledging and respecting grief

17 People with learning difficulties should be listened to and have opportunities to talk about their sadness.

18 A bereaved person should never be jollied along or be required to join in parties, dances and outings.

19 It should not be assumed that a person does not feel any grief because they cannot verbally express it.

20 If the bereaved person cannot speak their relatives or staff should talk to them about the death so they have the opportunity to hear spoken words of explanation, regret and sympathy. It can be helpful for them to hear expressed and answered the questions they cannot themselves put into words.

21 Angry and irritable behaviour shown by bereaved people living in residential care or attending a day centre should be responded to with sympathy rather than punishment as it is a normal reaction to loss.

22 Staff should not make snap judgements about whether a person is deeply grieved or not; it is normal for some people to hide their grief.

23 People experiencing several deaths within a few years or less should be given special consideration and it should be acknowledged that multiple losses take away confidence.

Remembering

24 The dead person should be referred to and spoken about.

25 The person with a learning difficulty should be told what is to happen to his family house, and

should take part in helping to sort out the belongings of deceased parents.

26   If a person has to go into residential care after a parent dies care should be taken not to throw away their possessions without permission: things that appear worn-out are sometimes very important.

27   The bereaved person may like to have a photograph of his deceased parents and former home enlarged and framed. This suggestion should be put to them.

28   The bereaved person may like a book of memories, containing photographs, cards, letters, mementoes. This may be comforting if the person has a speech difficulty.

29   Professionals may need to give help in buying a memorial stone for a parent's grave, or in getting a rose-bush planted in a garden of remembrance, or in putting an anniversary notice in the local newspaper. Suggestions and help should be offered with sensitivity.

30   The person who has a learning difficulty should be permitted to contribute to their parents' memorial stone or rose-bush, even if other relatives say that this is not necessary.

31   The person should be given opportunities to visit the cemetery or garden of remembrance, especially if they are speechless and/or immobile and cannot ask to go or get themselves there independently.

32   The anniversary of a person's death is important and should be remembered with respect and with reference to any happy memories as well as sad ones.

33   Bereaved people may need special loving atten-

tion at times of festivities – Christmas, Easter, birthdays – for at these times they are especially likely to be missing the dead person.

Better planning and kinder services

34 If a district has a register of people with learning difficulties this may be used to give a possible forecast of likely bereavements and thus enable some support plans to be made by local professionals and the families.

35 Local groups of parents and professionals and members of MENCAP, MIND, CRUSE and Compassionate Friends might find it helpful to meet occasionally to get to know each other and discuss issues of bereavement and how they might help each other.

36 Local social workers should be aware of the fact that some parents have never used services in caring for profoundly handicapped sons or daughters; when one of these parents dies the widow will be especially at risk of loneliness.

37 Local professionals and parents in some areas have written 'profiles' for people who have very severe learning difficulties; these will be very helpful if the person has no speech and is left alone after a widowed parent dies. The information on a profile should include the person's abilities, their likes and dislikes; their favourite foods, clothes, radio and TV programmes, games, music and books; the names and addresses of close relatives and friends; and details of daily routines such as dressing, bathing and mealtimes.

38 Immediate admission to residential care after the death of a widowed parent should be avoided. If possible the person should remain in their own

home for at least a few nights, with somebody staying with them, for example, a neighbour or relative, or friend, or an appointed student social worker or student nurse or volunteer.

39   Whether the person goes into residential care or remains in their own home their familiar routines of care should be continued, especially if they are profoundly handicapped.

40   Steps which are taken to prepare a young person for independence, such as leaving home for periods of short-term residential care, should only be organised if the short-term care is sensitively managed and appropriate for that person. It should not be assumed that short-term residential care is always a good experience of leaving home.

41   If a parent or friend or relative is very ill in a hospital or hospice the person with a learning difficulty should be given the same opportunities to say goodbye as other members of the family have. General hospital staff and hospice staff may need to have this spelt out to them if they have a stereotype image of people with learning difficulties.

42   Short-term residential care might not be the best arrangement when a parent is in hospital, as the short-term care unit may not be near the person's own home or near the hospital and it will be difficult for them to visit the ill parent. Perhaps arrangements could be made for them to stay in their own home with somebody staying with them if necessary and appropriate support services being arranged.

43   If going into residential care after a bereavement, the person should be able to take belongings, mementoes and photographs, from home; and

should have somewhere private and safe to keep them.

44 No person should be 'assessed' in the twelve months following a bereavement, for this will be a time when they will feel low and not able to do their best.

45 No person should have to endure two, three, four or more moves into different places of residential care following a bereavement.

46 Every effort should be made to let a person with a learning difficulty continue attending their familiar day centre after a bereavement, even if the death has meant their move into residential care outside that day centre's immediate 'catchment area'. This concession may need some special organisation regarding transport, but will mean that the bereaved person will not have to suffer the additional loss of their friends and staff of the day centre.

47 Widows left caring single-handed for a very severely multiply handicapped son or daughter should be linked as promptly as possible to the appropriate support services, which they may need on a temporary or permanent basis: for example, home helps, Meals-on-Wheels, a sitter service, help with shopping and transport.

48 Professionals should not try to entirely reorganise a family after a bereavement, nor impose on them more changes than they wish for or can cope with.

49 Widows on their own and confined to the house because they are caring for a son or daughter with severe multiple disabilities may like the moral support of visits from a social worker or a member of CRUSE if they have not got close relatives or known neighbours to talk to.

50   A person with a learning difficulty who is left
     alone and goes into residential care may have
     had a special friend amongst former neighbours;
     efforts should be made to find out about neighbour
     contacts to see if these can be maintained.

51   A person who is admitted to residential care
     because of a bereavement might find it helpful to
     have one member of staff taking a special interest
     in him.

52   Staff in day centres or residential units should
     give the bereaved person an opportunity to write
     thank you letters for flowers and condolences, and
     offer appropriate help with these letters if neces-
     sary.

53   A voluntary visitor may be helpful if a bereaved
     person in residential care has no relatives or
     friends who can visit. But care should be taken to
     ensure that the voluntary visitor does not start
     off with enthusiasm and then let the person down.

54   Efforts should be made to ensure that grieving
     persons living in residential care have access to
     quiet places where they can go at any time of the
     day if they wish to be private and sad.

55   All members of staff who come regularly into con-
     tact with a person living in a long-stay hospital
     (for example, porters, cleaners, therapy staff, doc-
     tors, teachers, psychologists, volunteers and
     administrators) should be informed if that person
     becomes bereaved. This will help to prevent tact-
     less remarks and will give an opportunity to
     express sympathy.

57   In long-stay hospitals it could be helpful for a
     small group of staff to take special responsibility
     for ensuring that:
     a) the needs of bereaved residents are being appro-

priately met according to their individual needs as long-stay residents or newly admitted residents, and b) individual members of staff are not being criticised for 'emotional involvement', but are themselves being supported in giving support to bereaved residents.

Deaths in long-stay hospitals

57 If a person who is living in a long-stay hospital becomes terminally ill they should remain in their own wards, if possible and if comfortable for them, and their friends should be permitted to see them and sit by them.

58 When a friend in a long-stay hospital dies, the other residents should be told and should be able to see the dead body if they wish to. There should be no indecent haste to take away the body and clear out the locker and erase all trace of the dead resident.

59 Staff should not select certain residents to tell about a death and certain ones not to tell or to lie to. All the residents should be told with honesty, even if the staff are worried about angry reactions or severe grief or think that some persons are too multiply handicapped to understand.

60 Opportunities should be given to attend the funeral of a dead resident and to contribute to flowers and send messages of condolence to the family.

61 The death of a member of staff should not be hushed up.

62 Staff should be aware of the special support needed by the very elderly residents of those wards in the long-stay hospital where a group of people may have been living together for many

years and are beginning to experience several
deaths a year amongst their friends in the ward.

63   The staff of wards where very elderly residents
are living are likely to need support from their
senior staff in coping with several deaths amongst
their residents within a short space of time.

Other forms of loss

64   When members of staff leave a school, day centre
or long-stay hospital, through retirement or going
to work elsewhere, their clients with learning difficulties may experience feelings of loss similar
to bereavement through a death. They should be
permitted to talk about missing that member of
staff, and they may be helped by receiving an
occasional visit or phone call or letter.

65   Memories of bad experiences of loss in childhood,
such as early loss of parents through going into
institutional care, may be activated by later losses
in adulthood such as moving into a different residential setting or a member of staff leaving. A
person's past history of losses and childhood deprivations should be acknowledged as a likely cause
of unhappiness in adulthood.

66   Moving from a long-stay hospital into a small
house or home after living for many years in hospital is a form of loss. The move should be care-
fully organised with adequate explanations and
preparation. Ample opportunity should be given
to say good-bye to all known staff and other residents.

67   A photograph of the hospital and staff and residents might be helpful when a person moves out.
Whatever shortcomings the hospital had it was

still the person's home for many years and their feelings of loss must be respected.

68 If somebody has left friends behind in the hospital every effort should be made to help them to keep in touch through letters, phone calls, messages and visits.

69 A pet dying can cause severe grief; this should be recognised and helped in a sympathetic manner.

Beware of rigid ideas

70 Professionals should take care not to make the subject of death 'trendy'.

71 It should be remembered that people vary, therefore it might not be very helpful to be too rigid about theories of 'stages of grief'.

72 Dead people are not mourned by everybody to the same extent — they may have actually been rather disliked, therefore a lot of grief should not be expected when in life there was some hostility.

73 It should never be assumed that people who have learning difficulties do not feel grief.

Conclusion

The question I always ask about research is: will it help anyone? The hope is that one's research will create some sort of positive change by giving a fresh angle to an old theory and asking questions of assumptions.

I particularly hope that this piece of work will help people to be more sensitive to their own potential for helping other people through times of sadness.

Regarding any further research, I hope that researchers who are interested in helping people and improving services might explore in more detail the following three findings which have come from my work:

One: How widows sometimes fantasise that their dead spouse is still alive (Chapter 2, pages 60–3);

Two: How people with learning difficulties are at risk of multiple moves following a bereavement (Chapter 3, pages 82–5);

Three: Multiple bereavements amongst elderly people living in long-stay mental handicap hospitals (Chapter 5, pages 133–4).

FURTHER READING

Non-fiction

BOWLBY, John, *Loss: Sadness and Depression* (Hogarth Press and the Institute of Psycho-analysis, London, 1980).

ENGLAND, Audrey (ed.), *Helping Ourselves*, excerpts from newsletters of the Compassionate Friends (Printed by Compassionate Friends, Bristol, 1985).

FLOWER, Dorothy, *Susan's Story*, a personal account of how a family faced a bereavement (The Royal Society for Mentally Handicapped Children and Adults, London, 1983).

GORER, Geoffrey, *Death, Grief and Mourning in Contemporary Britain* (Cresset Press, London, 1985).

MARRIS, Peter, *Widows and their Families* (Routledge & Kegan Paul, London, 1958).

MURRAY-PARKES, Colin, *Bereavement* (Tavistock Publications, London, 1972).

PINCUS, Lily, *Death and the Family* (Faber & Faber, London, 1976).

TOYNBEE, Arnold (ed.), *Man's Concern with Death* (Hodder & Stoughton, London, 1968).

WERTHEIMER, Alison, (1982) *Living for the Present*, CMH Enquiry Paper No 9 (Campaign for Mentally Handicapped People (Values Into Action), London, 1982).

Fiction

AGEE, James, *A death in the Family* (Quartet Books, London, 1980).

COOK, David, *Walter* (Penguin Books, London, 1978).

HILL, Susan, *In the Springtime of the Year* (Penguin Books, London, 1984).

Anthology

ENRIGHT, D. J. (ed.), *The Oxford Book of Death* (Oxford University Press, 1987).

Films

SIRELING, L. and HOLLINS, S., *The Last Taboo — Mental Handicap and Death*, a teaching video, 25 minutes (available from St George's Hospital Medical School, London, 1985).

WOHL, Ira, *Best Boy*, a film made by Ira Wohl of the USA on how his cousin Philly's life was changed by the death of his father (available from Concord Film Council, Ltd., 102 Felixstowe Road, Ipswich, Suffolk, 1979).

HELPFUL ORGANISATIONS

CRUSE, the national organisation for the widowed and their children, CRUSE House, 126 Sheen Road, Richmond, Surrey.

The Compassionate Friends, 6 Denmark Street, Bristol, BS1 5DQ.

National Association of Bereavement Services, 68 Chalton Street, London NW1 1JR.

MENCAP — The Royal Society for Mentally Handicapped Children and Adults, 123 Golden Lane, London EC1Y 0RT.

Down's Syndrome Association, 12–13 Clapham Common Southside, London SW4 7AA.

MIND, the National Association for Mental Health, 22 Harley Street, London W1N 2ED.

Spastics Society, 12 Park Crescent, London W1N 4EQ.

Values Into Action (VIA), Oxford House, Derbyshire Street, London E2 6HG.

In Touch Trust, mental handicap — parent contact organisation, 10 Norman Road, Sale, Cheshire, M33 3DF.

The National Autistic Society, 276 Willesden Lane, London NW2 5RB.

The Association for Spina Bifida and Hydrocephalus (Asbah), 42 Park Road, Peterborough PE1 2UQ.